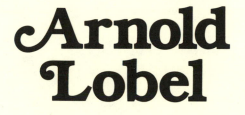

Arnold Lobel

Twayne's United States Authors Series
Children's Literature

Ruth K. MacDonald, Editor

TUSAS 552

ARNOLD LOBEL
Photograph reprinted by permission of the photographer, Adam Lobel.

Arnold Lobel

George Shannon

Twayne Publishers • Boston
A Division of G. K. Hall & Co.

Arnold Lobel
George Shannon

Twayne's United States Authors Series
Children's Literature/TUSAS 552

Copyediting supervised by Barbara Sutton.
Book production by Janet Z. Reynolds

Typeset in 10/13 Century Schoolbook
by Compset, Inc., Beverly, Massachusetts

Printed on permanent/durable acid-free paper
and bound in the United States of America

Library of Congress Cataloging-in-Publication Data

Shannon, George.
    Arnold Lobel / George Shannon.
        p.   cm.—(Twayne's United States authors series ; TUSAS
    552. Children's literature)
        Bibliography: p.
        Includes index.
        ISBN 0-8057-7544-7 (alk. paper)
        1. Lobel, Arnold—Criticism and interpretation. 2. Children's
    stories, American—History and criticism. I. Title. II. Series:
    Twayne's United States authors series ; TUSAS 552. III. Series:
    Twayne's United States authors series. Children's literature.
    PS3562.018Z87   1989
    813'.54—dc19   89-2106
                                                                        CIP

A novel is a garden carried in the pocket.

—Arabian proverb

Contents

Preface

In the field of children's literature Arnold Lobel is a rarity, acknowledged from all perspectives as one at the top of his profession. Lobel is modest, viewing himself as a "trained illustrator and a lucky amateur in terms of writing,"[1] but it is through his writing that he has given the most to readers and most deeply affected the field of children's literature. His work has been critically acclaimed since 1963 when *A Holiday for Mister Muster* was named one of the Best Illustrated Children's Books of the year by the *New York Times Book Review*. Significant succeeding awards include five more such honors from the *New York Times,* a Caldecott Medal, two Caldecott Honor Awards, and a Newbery Honor Award. In 1971 Lobel was a National Book Award finalist for *Frog and Toad Are Friends*. Lobel's craftsmanship and talent in book design, writing, and illustration have also made him respected by his peers. Finally—and too often not true of works by honored children's writers—Lobel's stories and characters are loved by children.

Despite all of this, little has been written to date on Lobel's work, and he has been noticeably excluded from several major surveys. In 1975, after only the first two volumes of their quartet had been published, Margery Fisher included Frog and Toad in *Who's Who in Children's Books: A Treasury of the Familiar Characters of Childhood*. Fisher wrote: "There can have been few writers since Beatrix Potter who use snatches of talk so subtly to indicate the human type within a true animal and few artists who so wittingly, meticulously and sympathetically suggest personality through the entirely natural movements of animals."[2] However, Margaret Blount's *Animal Land: The Creatures of Children's Fiction,* published the same year, does not mention Lobel at all.

Nor does Barbara Bader in *American Picturebooks: Noah's Ark to the Beast Within* (1976), which even features a chapter entitled "The Fabulists."

Ten years later, Helbig and Perkins also failed to include any of his works in their *Dictionary of American Children's Fiction, 1960–1984: Recent Books of Recognized Merit* (1986). The very volumes these studies have overlooked, primarily the *Frog and Toad* quartet, have, however, been honored by inclusion elsewhere. The photo-essay *The Family of Children* (1977) quotes from *Frog and Toad Are Friends,* and Gareth Matthews discusses a *Frog and Toad* story in each of his two volumes on children and philosophy, *Philosophy and the Young Child* (1980) and *Dialogues with Children* (1984), as excellent examples of what he calls "philosophical whimsy." *Twentieth-Century Children's Writers* (1983) states: "In the field of the contemporary picturebook, Arnold Lobel has clearly emerged as a significant writer . . . his works contain two of those timeless qualities which have traditionally defined classic works of children's literature: humor and truth."[3]

This study of Lobel's work is offered as a window on his books through which others may come to see even more. I have also written it knowing that no matter what is said about Lobel the best of his books will live on without assistance from academia as classics always do.

Leaving basic history to the Chronology, chapter 1 is a biography of Lobel's pastoral voice as reflected in both his fiction and his daily life. The uniqueness and completeness of his voice has brought renewed energy to the field of children's literature and joy to his readers. This coexistence of life and bookmaking can be traced to the late fifties when Lobel began work as a children's book illustrator. Though he was to become one of his generation's finest writers, he continued to illustrate texts by others throughout his career. Chapter 2 explores his growth as an illustrator with an emphasis on his outstanding work in the early-reader genre and his cinematic use of framed images. Chapter 3 examines his texts of the early sixties that, in retrospect, can be seen as rehearsals for *Frog and Toad.*

Throughout Lobel's life Edward Lear was one of his favorite

writer-illustrators and a nurturing influence on his work. Their most obvious connection is Lobel's *Book of Pigericks* (1983), yet most of his books from the late sixties through his final book, *The Turnaround Wind* (1988), are related to Lear to some degree. Chapter 4 explores Lear's sense of visual and verbal nonsense as reflected in Lobel's work and especially how this was transformed through Lobel's pastoral perspective to become his own.

If he had written only his four volumes of *Frog and Toad* stories he would still be a significant name in twentieth-century children's literature, a position enhanced by his five other "I Can Read" texts of the seventies. Chapter 5 discusses Frog and Toad as archetypal pastoral characters, the depth of their stories, and their literary connections with Beatrix Potter and Kenneth Grahame. While *Frog and Toad* are pastoral stories containing nonsense, *Mouse Tales* and *Mouse Soup* are nonsense stories that evoke a pastoral mood. Both are examined in chapter 7. *Owl at Home, Grasshopper on the Road,* and *Uncle Elephant* complete Lobel's collection of "I Can Read" texts, and chapter 8 explores these volumes as Lobel's autobiographical triptych.

Like the early pastoralist Theocritus,[4] Lobel absorbed a great deal of folk literature into his work. His use and unique extension of the fable, most particularly in *Fables,* is the focus of chapter 6. Just as the pastoral is the core of his "I Can Read" texts, Mother Goose is the heart of Lobel's picture books of the late seventies and early eighties. Chapter 9 examines his growth as a folk-style narrator and his sense of verse and rhyme as pastoral song.

The writing of this book was greatly aided by Arnold Lobel's warm invitations to visit with him in person and by phone during what became the final year of his life. Also of encouraging support and assistance were Anita Lobel, Adam Lobel, Elizabeth Gordon, Susan Hirschman, Charlotte Zolotow, Bill Morris, Barbara Dicks, Ava Weiss, and John Wallowitch. I also extend my thanks to the staffs of the McIntyre Library at the University of Wisconsin–Eau Claire, the Philips Memorial Library, the Kerlan Collection, and the de Grummond Collection with special thanks to Dee Jones.

I am deeply appreciative of the catalytic criticism given me on this project by my Twayne editors Ruth MacDonald and Liz Traynor, and by my friend and colleague, Virginia Wolf. Not only did Virginia suggest this project, but our long Frog-and-Toad–style walks set much of this book to growing. As Lobel knew, laughter and love are two of the most sustaining forces in our lives, and for these I eagerly thank Carol Schumacher, Dakota Fox, Kate McIntyre, Anne McConnell, and, especially, David Holter.

George Shannon

Eau Claire, Wisconsin

Acknowledgments

I would like to thank the following publishers and Adam Lobel representing the Estate of Arnold Lobel for granting permission to reprint excerpts from the following works:

The Bears in the Air, © 1965; *The Book of Pigericks,* © 1983; *Days with Frog and Toad,* © 1979; *Fables,* © 1980; *Frog and Toad All Year,* © 1976; *Frog and Toad Are Friends,* © 1970; *Frog and Toad Together,* © 1972; *Grasshopper on the Road,* © 1978; *The Great Blueness and Other Predicaments,* © 1968; *The Man Who Took the Indoors Out,* © 1974; *Martha, the Movie Mouse,* © 1966; *Mouse Soup,* © 1977; *Mouse Tales,* © 1972; *Owl at Home,* © 1975; *The Turnaround Wind,* © 1988; *Uncle Elephant,* © 1981; and *A Zoo for Mister Muster,* © 1962. All reprinted by permission of Harper & Row.

Whiskers & Rhymes, © 1985. Reprinted by permission of Greenwillow Books (a Division of William Morrow & Company, Inc).

The Ice-Cream Cone Coot and Other Rare Birds, © 1971. Reprinted by permission of Scholastic, Inc.

"The Evening Meal," in *The Scribner Anthology for Young People,* edited by Anne Diven, © 1976. Reprinted by permission of Charles Scribner's Sons, an imprint of Macmillan Publishing Company.

"A Rabbit Song" (unpublished manuscript). Reprinted by permission of the Estate of Arnold Lobel.

The following publishers also granted permission to reprint illustrations from these works:

The Book of Pigericks, © 1983; *Frog and Toad Are Friends,* © 1970; *The Man Who Took the Indoors Out,* © 1974; *Mouse Soup,*

Chronology

1933 Arnold (Stark) Lobel born 22 May in Los Angeles, California. Six months later his parents, Joseph and Lucille (Stark) Lobel move back to Schenectady, New York, and divorce soon after. Arnold lives in Schenectady with his mother and maternal grandparents until he begins college at Pratt Institute in Brooklyn.

1955 Earns B.F.A. from Pratt Institute; marries fellow student Anita Kempler. Continues living in Brooklyn and begins work with various advertising agencies. Daughter Adrianne born.

1958 Publishes first illustrations with Ktav for three activity books by Sol Scharfstein: *Bibletime, Hebrew Dictionary,* and *Holiday Dictionary.*

1959 Son Adam born.

1961 Illustrates *Red Tag Comes Back* by Fred Phlegar, first book with Harper & Row.

1962 Writes and illustrates his first text, *A Zoo for Mister Muster.*

1963 *A Holiday for Mister Muster,* which is named a Best Illustrated Children's Book by the *New York Times Book Review. Prince Bertram the Bad.*

1964 Writes and illustrates first "I Can Read" text, *Lucille. Giant John.*

1965 *The Bears of the Air.*

1966 *Martha, the Movie Mouse.*

1968 *The Great Blueness and Other Predicaments.*

1969 *Small Pig.*

1970 *Frog and Toad Are Friends* wins Caldecott Honor Award, is Children's National Book Award finalist.

1971 Illustrates *Hildilid's Night* by Cheli D. Ryan, which wins Caldecott Honor Award is National Book Award finalist and selected for Children's Book Showcase. *The Ice Cream Cone Coot and Other Rare Birds. On the Day Peter Stuyvesant Sailed into Town* also selected for Children's Book Showcase.

1972 *Frog and Toad Together* wins Newbery Honor Award and selected for Children's Book Showcase. *Mouse Tales* wins Irma Simonton Black Award for Excellence in Children's Literature. *Seahorse* selected for Children's Book Showcase.

1973 Illustrates *The Clay Pot Boy* by Cynthia Jameson selected for Children's Book Showcase.

1974 *The Man Who Took the Indoors Out* is named a Best Illustrated Children's Book by the *New York Times Book Review* and also selected for the Children's Book Showcase. Illustrates *Miss Suzy's Birthday* by Miriam Young, also named a Best Illustrated Children's Book by the *New York Times Book Review*.

1975 *Owl at Home.* Illustrates *As I Was Crossing Boston Common* by Norma Farber, a National Book Award finalist and selected for the Children's Book Showcase.

1976 *Frog and Toad All Year.* Illustrates *As Right as Right Can Be* by Anne Rose, which is named a Best Illustrated Children's Book by the *New York Times Book Review*. Illustrates *Nightmares: Poems to Trouble Your Sleep* by Jack Prelutsky selected for the Children's Book Showcase.

1977 *Mouse Soup. How the Rooster Saved the Day* illustrated by Anita Lobel. Illustrates *Merry Merry FIBruary* by Doris Orgel, which is named a Best Illustrated Children's Book by the *New York Times Book Review.*

1978 *Grasshopper on the Road. Gregory Griggs and Other Nursery Rhyme People.* Receives George G. Stone Award from Claremont College for his *Frog and Toad* series.

1979 *Days with Frog and Toad. A Treeful of Pigs* illustrated by Anita Lobel.

1980 *Fables* wins Caldecott Award. Illustrates *The Headless Horseman Rides Tonight* by Jack Prelutsky, which is named a Best Illustrated Children's Book by the *New York Times Book Review.*

1981 *Ming Lo Moves the Mountain. Uncle Elephant. On Market Street* illustrated by Anita Lobel.

1983 *The Book of Pigericks.*

1984 *The Rose is My Garden* illustrated by Anita Lobel. Moves from Brooklyn to Manhattan.

1985 *Whiskers & Rhymes.* Receives University of Southern Mississippi Medallion for Distinguished Service to Children's Literature.

1986 *The Random House Book of Mother Goose.*

1987 Illustrates cover for *Horn Book Magazine.* Dies 4 December at Doctors Hospital in Manhattan.

1988 *The Turnaround Wind.*

1

Telling One's Way to Arcadia

> . . . if they wish to do something nice for me, ask them to look at the books. Because that's where they'll find me.[1]

Like his literary ancestor, Aesop, Arnold Lobel grew up as an outsider. And, as it did for Aesop, turning life's foibles into stories allowed him to move from the outside in. Lobel always loved books, but a pair of "portentous wet feet" in the first grade was the first step toward dissolving barriers through telling stories:

> . . . the wet feet turned into a bad cold, the bad cold turned into an ear infection, the ear infection became a mastoid, and I was shunted off to the hospital for an operation and six months of recovery in the hospital followed by six slow months of convalescence at home. The upshot of all this horror of horrors was that I missed the entire second grade. There was a kind of balcony-sunporch arrangement on the hospital, which, ironically enough, overlooked the schoolyard where I should have been, and I stood there watching my friends coming in and out, playing at recess, and so forth, and felt a great loneliness, a great longing and separation.[2]

Lobel went back to the third grade the following year but found none of the joy he had envisioned. While he was still printing his letters with a fat pencil everyone else was writing in script with thin pencils. Tutoring helped the writing, but not the image. Former friends now viewed him as a "kind of freak, stranger, a certain social outcast."[3] Skinny and bespectacled, he hadn't a chance of proving his worth on the playground or in the gym and was even beaten up.

Then one afternoon when his teacher was at a loss to fill the final minutes of class, she asked if anyone would like to tell a story or some personal experience. Arnold raised his hand:

> Bravely I walked to the front of the class. I could hear snickers up and down the rows behind me. Well, I told a story. I made it up out of my head as I went along. To my enormous surprise, the story had plot, characterization, dialogue; I picked up a piece of chalk and drew on the blackboard—the story had illustration. . . . I was a smash. Scheherazade had needed a thousand and one nights of tales to save her life. I had done it in one afternoon in one fell swoop. There was a clamorous demand for frequent stories from me. The class was enthralled, and I was elevated to a position of high social esteem which lasted for a couple of years, until I myself put a stop to it.[4]

While Lobel felt the need to leave storytelling behind as he entered adolescence, story in one form or another continued to be his emotional pleasance, just as it had been in the third grade and even earlier when he would sit with a fresh supply of library books beneath the front-yard tree.

While chronology establishes what Lobel did and when and where, the stories he wrote, loved to read, and those he told of himself (like the one above) tell much more about who he was. "The events of a story may have much or little to do with the writer's own life," states Eudora Welty in *The Eye of the Story,* "but the pattern is the nearest thing to a mirror image of his heart

and mind."[5] These patterns, the thematic concerns of his characters, and the imagery he used instinctively, provide the truest
sense of who Lobel was, revealing the channels of his thought and
the objects and incidents he observed and remembered. The essence within all of these is the same—that of the pastoral
interlude.

Playing the Shepherd's Flute

Though the pastoral genre was initially identified by its content—shepherd, flute, and shade tree or grove—it has evolved to
include all literature that evokes the mood of that early image,
whether shepherds appear or not. It is the world and mood that
artist-illustrator Henri Matisse, a favorite of Lobel's, sought to
create in his work: "an art of balance, of purity and serenity, de-
void of troubling or depressing subject matter, an art which could
be for every mental worker, for the businessman as well as the
man of letters, for example, a soothing, calming influence on the
mind, something like a good armchair which provides relaxation
from physical fatigue."[6]

The pastoral is the quintessential "time away" where no questions are asked, no judgments made, everyone is equal, and no
one ages. The primary objective of the pastoral grove is that of
liberation.[7] Song and gentle laughter fill the air and when one
does leave, he does so refreshed and enamored of life. It is, no
matter what creates it, a miniature world of renewal or, as Bachelard calls it in *The Poetics of Space,* "felicitous space."[8]

In periods of history the pastoral landscape of meadow, grove,
and/or garden came to symbolize the pastoral world of Arcadia.
For Lobel, the pastoral mood was symbolized by the home and all
it included. The warm pleasures of his childhood home—"a nice
house with nice furniture, a nice backyard with trees and everything,"[9] including his grandfather's garden—was expanded time
and again in both his adult homes and in his illustrations. Home
in both life and fiction was where Lobel most liked to be. "I'm
really a very domestic person. I guess that comes through in the

illustrations, in most of my work. It's all very bourgeois. There's a lot of furniture, a lot of accoutrements of the home, because that's what I am."[10]

While the home of Bellwood Bouse in *The Man Who Took the Indoors Out* is Lobel's fullest house, the essence of his home as Arcadia can be found in his "I Can Read" books. The visual world of Frog and Toad is the pastoral as absorbed and transformed by cultures of northern climates. "The garden," states Blue Calhoun in *The Pastoral Vision of William Morris: The Earthly Paradise,* "is momentarily transformed into the interior shelter of hearth, warm drink, tale-telling, and fellowship."[11]

Fireside tale-telling or reading in Lobel's world is itself Arcadian and synonymous with the act of friendship. When Toad is reading to Frog or Frog is telling a story to Toad, they are literally co-creating the story and are closer than at other times. In the innocence of Arcadia sharing stories is a sensual act. As Faye Leeper discusses in "Talking and Touching: A Function of Storytelling," storytelling offers a substitute for direct physical contact and exists as the most "ideally socially acceptable event for consummating the desire for being close to other human beings."[12] Sharing tales by the fireplace, Frog and Toad are cultured versions of the archetypal boys sitting close to one another, sharing stories in their treehouse the summer of their eleventh year.

Believing as he did that the act of reading (especially of reading picture books) provides a pastoral interlude or form of felicitous space, it is not surprising that one of Lobel's frequent images is that of a character reading a book beneath a tree or in a plump armchair. He also describes good picture books as pastoral. "They are objects of pleasing self-containment, somehow capable of suggesting everything that is good about feeling well and having positive thoughts about being alive. They're filled with light and color."[13]

This tone is also expressed in Lobel's visual approach or attitude toward his illustrations and his readers. Place his books alongside others, even others of similar subject matter or genre, and Lobel's reveal their quietness and sense of gentle invitation. There is a sense of nearness in his illustrations that establishes

From *The Man Who Took the Indoors Out* by Arnold Lobel. © 1974 by Arnold Lobel. Reprinted by permission of Harper & Row, p. 4. Photographed from the artist's original pen and ink drawing: 19.8 cm × 15.5 cm.

the story's world as one just beyond the reader's toes. While others present their picture-book worlds as panoramas or fields of vigorous movement, Lobel shares his with a gardenlike size and gesture. The reader can watch the visual worlds of illustrators such as Paul Goble, Paul Galdone, and the Dillons, but one senses he can actually enter the world of Frog and Toad. Lobel belongs, to borrow Hilda van Stockum's phrase in describing Leslie Brooke of *Johnny Crow's Garden,* to the "Come-gather-around-and-I'll-tell-you-a-story" school of illustration.[14] Rather than bouncing out to meet the reader (his *Mother Goose* is a vibrant exception), Lobel's books wait with a quiet sureness and draw the reader inside.

Books also became the Arcadian garden that Lobel entered time and time again for his own creative nourishment. "At some point in my career, I made the decision that to create books for children was to live a life of necessary isolation. . . . Inspiration was to be found not in the noisy and unpredictable company of children, but in the safe, dark confines of my imagination, among the dusty pages of my book collection."[15] This reflective and contemplative approach to work and reading allowed Lobel to live the epigraph of one of his favorite children's books, *Rain Rain Rivers* by Uri Shulevitz: "Without going out of my door / I know the universe."[16]

Pastoral characters, like the classic shepherd, are primarily sensualists and possess little self-awareness. They have no need to analyze life. They live instead to share their world with friends and celebrate all of life by creating songs, poems, and, more recently, stories about it. Theirs is an adult's world of freedom, but with its burdens replaced by a child's sense of play; in other words, everyone's holiday, honeymoon, and retirement home rolled into one.

Sharing the pastoral song with friends—active companionship—is the core of Arcadian freedom or liberation. "Come now," wrote Theocritus in his seventh Idyll, "we share the walk, we share the morning; Strike up the pastoral song; one will support the other."[17] Such companionships were also the core of Lobel's life off and on the printed page.

Long before he befriended frogs and toads in Vermont and began to create stories of Arcadian friendship, Lobel was writing of companionship. Mister Muster feels a friendship with the zoo animals, and they with him. *Lucille, Small Pig, Prince Bertram,* and *Giant John* all explore, in part, evolving friendships. And most dramatically, Martha, the movie mouse, befriends Dan the projectionist and eventually the entire theater audience by telling stories. Lobel's books of the seventies formed a growing ode to friendship in all its variations. Bellwood Bouse loves the objects that make his house a home and misses their companionship when they leave him, and Uncle Elephant and his nephew share the best of intergenerational friendships. Frog and Toad are pastoral equals, and Owl is friend to moon, extending Lobel's belief that being a friend is itself a gift or, as he states in his moral to "The Ostrich in Love" in *Fables,* "Love can be its own reward (7)."

Lobel's appreciation for friendship is also reflected in his stopping the Frog and Toad stories with the fourth volume. Rather than allowing their friendship to become a commodity or be taken for granted he chose to stop and keep their relationship more alive by narrowing the time span, thus increasing the vitality of their time together. Though completely instinctual, Lobel's own published remarks as to why he was stopping the stories show that in his own eyes more stories would have only tarnished their pastoral relationship. It "occurred to me, when I was doing the last one, that there was a certain cruelty in the relationship, in Frog being the controlling one and Toad being controlled."[18] Such changes, if explored in their stories, would have ended their pastoral friendship because the basic premises of living in the Arcadian garden or grove would have been destroyed: amiability, courtesy, and intimacy without deference.[19]

Like Walt Whitman's in *Leaves of Grass,* Lobel's understanding of companionship or comradeship is broad and encompassing. Both family and friendship were, or could be, Arcadian gardens. Focusing as he did on child-substitute characters, Lobel has few traditional families in his stories, but those he has celebrate the same pastoral joy of companionship as Frog and Toad.

The text of Lobel's single completed and submitted, yet unpublished manuscript, "A Rabbit Song" (around 1976), is an ode to the warmth of family. While many of his other stories conclude with the protagonist going home to supper, "A Rabbit Song" begins with "A rabbit was on his way home to supper." Along the way he sings a riddle song about once having none, but now many. Various animals along his path guess, but fail to figure out what has increased that makes him sing so joyfully. Once home, rabbit opens his door and soon everyone knows the answer. "'CHILDREN IS RIGHT!' said the rabbit and they all ran out to kiss their father hello."[20] Here, as in *Uncle Elephant* and *Mouse Tales,* family evokes the heart of pastoral friendship, joy, and acceptance.

In responding to Lee Bennett Hopkins's questionnaire for *Books Are by People* (1969), Lobel wrote "I also get much comfort from the companionship of my wife and a few close friends."[21] It was a companionship beautifully illustrated on the final page of *Mouse Tales.* With the children lulled to sleep by stories, momma and papa mouse, depicted as Anita and Arnold, share a quiet pastoral moment of tea and conversation by the fireplace.

It was after their own young children had gone to bed that the young Lobels would begin their artistic work in earnest. Working on a door they had turned into a table, Arnold and Anita would draw and jiggle (and often quibble over the jiggling) far into the night. In time, they created separate tables and eventually had a studio room. But no matter the size of their living quarters, they always kept their drawing tables side by side or facing each other. "We're two flying buttresses," Anita said in 1981, "supporting the work we are both doing in the room."[22]

The early eighties, however, brought many changes to the Lobels' lives including separate moves from their Victorian row house in Brooklyn, with Anita moving to SoHo and Arnold to Greenwich Village on Washington Square. The time of transition was fraught with confusion, hurt, and anger, but their long friendship survived, evolved, and continued to buttress them both, though their drawing tables were then many blocks apart, and others had entered their romantic lives. Like Frog and Toad in their final story, they remained two close friends, alone and yet together.

Together constantly as a young family, the Lobels lived a mod-

From *Mouse Tales* by Arnold Lobel. © 1972 by Arnold Lobel. Reprinted by permission of Harper & Row, p. 64. Photographed from the artist's original pen and ink drawing with gray wash: 8 cm × 10 cm.

ern version of an agrarian life with both parents working at home and caring for the children. Their shared life was one of ongoing creativeness, idleness or pastoral play. Their son, Adam, worked with music, film, and photography. Their daughter, Adrianne, drew and eventually became a set designer. Anita wrote and illustrated picture books but also made time for needlepoint, stained glass, dance lessons, and occasional acting and cabaret singing. Arnold wrote a great deal and illustrated even more, extending his creations to needlepoint pillows of fantastic animals.

All of Lobel's characters fill their days with such creative idleness and share the delight of living apart from the clank and clash of cities and crowds. Even Martha who lives in the cold big city in *Martha, the Movie Mouse* finds a warm pastoral oasis of light and color when she moves into the movie theater. In time, she becomes a pastoral artist herself by turning the sad times of her life into poetry and song. Sharing stories, she finds not only the joy of creation, but also friendship and acceptance, just as Lobel had done in the third grade. And true to the timeless nature of the pastoral, none of Lobel's major characters regardless of their chronological age will ever grow beyond their eleventh year.

The paradox of the pastoral genre is that, free of questions, insight, and self-analysis, the classic pastoral character would never be able to create a pastoral work of art. It is instead the sophisticate of the city, who can see the contrasts of city and country and celebrate the balanced garden between the two, who creates the richest pastoral works. The pastoral has the genre's required "simple" voice, but as William Empson points out in *Some Versions of Pastoral,* it takes the writer of insight to put the complex into that simple voice.[23]

Though he visited the countryside, Lobel wrote his masterful pastoral stories as a city resident rather than as a country gentleman. Lobel chose to live his entire adult life in the city, first in Brooklyn, then in Greenwich Village, but choosing an address with windows on a park.

His homes held the essence of the pastoral world as symbolized in his 1987–88 cover for the *Horn Book* and most of his picture books. There is the dapper anthropomorphized cat in his much-loved home. The freshness of flowers. The joy of song. The warmth and light of the fireplace and the love of books and reading. There is even the nonsense, the laughter, of a house made out of books, and the truth of that image. Books and reading created for Lobel a pastoral world or home throughout his life. "When I am brought low by the vicissitudes of life, I stumble to my bookshelves. I take a little dose of Zemach or Shulevitz. I grab a shot of Goffstein or Marshall. I medicate myself with Steig or Sendak, and the treatment works. I always feel much better."[24]

Re-creating this pastoral interlude, as it was for Matisse,

became Lobel's creative goal. "I make a conscious attempt," he told *Instructor* in 1981, "to pull the child away from his or her environment. I think a child wants to read for escape."[25] Although he preferred to call himself an entertainer, Lobel's sense of escape was not one of avoidance, but of what Christopher Fry describes as the humorist's "escape into faith."[26] It is the escape to growth and renewal that is the heart of the pastoral world.

Answers as to why Lobel was drawn to the pastoral are as mercurial as the genre itself. Two primary threads stand out; however, they are so tightly braided, each is half the other. One is his role as outsider, the other, his innate sense of humor.

The story of Lobel's early grade school years and long illness well establish his position, or felt position, as an outsider. While in the hospital, he literally existed outside his peers' world, seeing them only through glass and at a distance. Though he was happy at home as a child, his family had to have made him feel different from peers. When he was very young and long before it was common, Arnold's parents divorced. He was raised by his grandmother, "who could cope with any crisis,"[27] and his much older grandfather while his mother went to work every day. His father was in California.

An additional element in his seeing the world as an outsider was his homosexuality, which he came to acknowledge in later life. By simply being who he was, Lobel existed, as do all minorities, outside the mainstream. And, whether acknowledged or not, the distance is felt and affects one's daily life, for society's lack of an affirming mirror creates a continual sense of exclusion.

When placed on the outside for whatever reason, one can either focus on the difference and do battle and intensify the wall of division while trying to overpower it, or one may dismantle it from within by finding more similarities than differences between those on the inside and out. Angry and combative, writers in battle are most often satiric or ironic in voice, if humorous at all. Those in the latter group, like Lobel, are by their perspective drawn to a voice that celebrates life in all its coexisting, albeit conflicting, forms, or, in other words, they are drawn to the pastoral genre.

Lobel's memories of humor in his youth were ones directly related to the pastoral interlude brought by home, story, and reading. Though his grandparents of German Jewish descent were stoic and reserved, Lobel remembered their home as filled with laughter but never tears. Two of the few childhood books he remembered into adulthood were also filled with laughter, *The 500 Hats of Bartholomew Cubbins* by Dr. Seuss and the freewheeling limericks of Edward Lear. Both were comic celebrations of incongruity, also a primary element of the pastoral.

As an adult Lobel continued to enjoy Lear and believed that humor *was* a pastoral world where child and adult could exist as equals. It "seems to me the one thing that doesn't change much as we grow older is our sense of humor. I think a child's sense of humor and an adult's sense of humor are rather the same. . . . We laugh at incongruity and we laugh at lack of dignity. If a man's pants fall down, everybody laughs, children, adults."[28]

With humor a common bond between child and adult, Lobel also saw it as a way to avoid the condescending sentimentality that ruins so many children's books. With the creation of stuffed Frog and Toad dolls bordering on the precious, Lobel found pleasure in the dolls falling victim to one of comedy's classic gags of lost dignity. "Their pants kept falling down in the early mockups," he told the *New York Times Book Review* in 1979, "but they've fixed that."[29] Vulnerable and subject to human comedy, the stuffed dolls bypassed sentimentality to become every one's equal. As this incident reveals, the tone of humor Lobel most appreciated and felt marked his best work was not coy or sweet, but an "agreeable combination of comedy and cantankerousness"[30]— the voices of Frog and Toad combined.

During Lobel's "bumpy adolescence"[31] the nonsense humor of the *Kuklapolitan Players* on WRGB-TV was a beloved pastoral interlude every afternoon. "I prolonged my childhood as long as possible, and the time with Kukla and Ollie was really the most important part of the day, all through high school."[32] Featuring the day-to-day activities of practical Kukla, doleful Ollie (both puppets), and their human friend Fran, the Kuklapolitans performed a wide range of productions from *The Mikado* to satires like *Martin Dragon, Private Tooth*. Joyful nonsense filled their world with Beulah Witch, a former electronics student, who flew jet-propelled brooms; Cecil Bill, their stage manager, who had a language all his own; and Ollie's mother, Olivia, whose hair was seventy-five feet long. At one point the creator of the Kuklapolitan puppets, Burr Tillstrom, visited Schenectady, and Lobel obtained a treasured photograph of Tillstrom and himself together.

Like Lobel's own Frog and Toad some twenty years later, the male friendship of Kukla and Ollie with their contrasting personalities, clever dialogue, and gentle humor, based on the absurd, echoes the classic pastoral idyll of shepherds near the shade tree.

Many of Lobel's early books including *A Zoo for Mister Muster, Lucille, The Bears of the Air,* and *Small Pig* are humorous tales that talk about the values of a pastoral life-style, but beginning with *Frog and Toad Are Friends* in 1970, the pastoral became Lobel's primary setting, the heart of his stories, influencing the effect his stories had on his readers.

After years of admiring the work of E. B. White, also a pastoralist, it was as if Lobel actually began living Stuart Little's advice to students: "Summer is important. It's like a shaft of sunlight. . . . Never forget your summers, my dears."[33] The conundrum of coincidence and / or cause and effect found Lobel in the late sixties growing displeased with the nature of his work at the same time that his children began growing out of childhood. Both situations sent his thoughts back to the summer of 1966 and, in true pastoral style,[34] brought a solution to his literary problem.

In order to escape the gritty heat and din of the city Lobel and his family rented an A-frame house on the shores of Lake Bomoseen in southern Vermont. The children "made of the lake and the woods and the whole surrounding countryside a wonderland, a golden summer of childhood experiences. I watched this with a kind of combination of vicarious pleasure and parental apprehension. I was always amazed to see them coming home at night undamaged and undrowned."[35] There were, of course, horrors and disappointments, but it was a vibrant time for his children and a glorious time of sharing with them. Part of that sharing involved the care and observation of pets, most particularly the frogs and toads discovered in nearby woods and swamps.

While he felt that parenthood often takes away some of what is creative in an artist, Lobel's view of parenthood helped in time to nourish his best work. In creating a pastoral life for his children he in a way gave one to himself. As he said, "After awhile it becomes second nature."[36] It was, then, not merely the passing of Adrianne and Adam's childhood that sent Lobel to remembering that summer in Vermont (and a second one as well), but also the passing of his role in their childhood.

By that point, he wrote, "all the disasters of the summer had faded into a sort of roseate glow. . . . And of course I thought about the frogs and the toads and how much I liked them, and I picked up my ballpoint writing pen and I wrote on the notebook, 'Frog ran up the path to Toad's house.' Well, the little stories just seemed to pour right out of me, and after two weeks, I knew that somehow I had come a little bit closer to being the kind of children's writer that I wanted to be."[37]

By the end of the decade Lobel's work in the pastoral had become so recognized for its thorough vision and quality that the genre within Lobel's time period had become synonymous with his name. He had truly created a world apart, a world or vision epitomized by Toad in "The Garden" in *Frog and Toad Together*. It was a world of friendship and comedy, obsession and gentleness, foolishness and thoughtfulness, in which story, song, and laughter were the greatest gifts. Every aspect of his work had become an intuitive note on the shepherd's reed flute.

Theater and Film

Lobel's pastoral interlude of story was not confined to storytelling and books. From his childhood he saw story, film, and theater as one. The cellar of his childhood home in Schenectady was often turned into a theater with the help of painted bedsheets, as Lobel acted out stories for friends. At school (most likely away from the teacher's ear), he told classmates how he had played with Shirley Temple, Mickey Rooney, and Judy Garland while living in California. While it was true that he had been born near Hollywood, young Arnold had moved back to Schenectady at the age of six months without once getting to play with any famous child stars.

This lie about Hollywood playmates was so desirable that Lobel came to believe it himself and, in retrospect, felt that it was through believing his own lie that he learned to become an artist. "Early on I learned to turn my lies into true self-illusion. I believed, and was able to make others believe—the prerequisite for any successful creative activity."[38]

Story as film and theater continued to be important in Lobel's life even after he had stopped telling stories to his classmates. He enjoyed movies at the Erie Theater, worked with high school plays, and treasured the theatrics of the *Kuklapolitan Players* on television.

Lobel continued to work with theater while attending art school at Pratt Institute in Brooklyn. He both directed and acted in several plays including *The Man Who Came to Dinner* and *Antigone*. Though Anita Kempler first "met" Arnold through his paintings, she got to know her future husband and he her when he directed her in Chekhov's one-act comedy, *The Marriage Proposal*. At the time Anita was more interested in Arnold than he in her, but during their summer apart Arnold began to miss her and started writing letters. They were married after graduating from Pratt.

Through his career Lobel's favorite metaphors when speaking of picture books were those of theater and film. While both clearly resemble the dual world of word and image found in picture books, they also represent personally ordered worlds or gardens that exist outside the clash and clank. "It is a kind of pleasant omnipotence that I feel at the drawing board. There is a little world at the end of my pencil. I am the stage director, the costume designer, and the man who pulls the curtain. If I'm in the mood, I can admit to being despotic, too, for when a character is not behaving as I would wish him to he can be quickly dismissed with a wave of my eraser. This is certainly part of the joy of making books for children."[39]

Working side by side for most of their careers, Arnold and Anita naturally fed one another's work through common approaches, friendship, and simple proximity. Both saw picture books as extensions of theater, yet each also maintained a distinctive version of that view. While Arnold's work was often drawn with a strong sense of audience and stage, as in *The Comic Adventures of Old Mother Hubbard* and *Someday* by Zolotow, Anita was more inclined to include visual elements of the stage itself, as with the curtains in *How the Rooster Saved the Day.*

Theater and film shaped the Lobels' lives away from the book page as well. In the late seventies Anita began acting again, including performing the lead in Robinson Jeffers's off-Broadway production of *Medea* in 1977. The advent of video brought endless tapes into the Lobel household and allowed Lobel to enjoy his love of home and film at the same time. Daughter Adrianne was becoming a busy and well-respected set designer, whose work includes Peter Sellars's production of *Nixon in China.* Mathew Anden, Lobel's friend and companion in later years, was also involved in theater and film as an actor until his death in 1985.

There are always multiple reasons that different people are drawn to the theater. While no single connection excludes any others, Paul Binding's study of poet and playwright Federico Garcia Lorca's relationship with theater and puppet theater would seem also to describe Lobel's. "Perhaps," states Binding, "the interplay of archetypes [in theater] has a life-enhancing allure for those who find the traffic of the persona difficult and oppressive."[40] In other words, dealing with the essence of the human condition, the theater exists outside of divisive details and as such becomes another variation on the pastoral interlude or pleasance.

Nearly fifty years after Lobel dazzled classmates with his tales of Hollywood playtimes, he did enter the world of movies by narrating John Matthews's excellent film version of *Frog and Toad Are Friends,* released in 1985. *Frog and Toad Together* followed in 1986 (though Lobel did not do the narration), and one of his final legal acts was to sign the papers allowing Matthews and Churchill Films to begin work on a film version of *Uncle Elephant,* in which Uncle Elephant introduces his nephew to the joys of the pastoral interlude.

Order

In addition to tranquility, innocence, and simplicity, the pastoral mood evokes a sense of things in order,[41] the garden's gentle design rather than the forest's chaos. Lobel's three major literary forms are closely tied to order and, in turn, are pastoral in experience. The "I Can Read" books, nonsense verse, and folklore are all grounded in an order that makes the unknown safe. The "I Can Read" will be mastered no matter what the story or new words. The nonsense verse will rhyme no matter how absurd its content, and the heroes of folklore will always triumph no matter what the conflicts. This juxtaposition of seeming chaos and order heightens the humor and sense of release of the characters' absurd behavior. Nonsense is also, states Fred Miller Robinson, "simultaneously an escape from and an affirmation or declaration of the orderly, the ordinary."[42] Thus all Lobel's literary forms create a pastoral interlude that allows the reader to relax, often laugh, and then return to his world renewed and refreshed.

A similar sense of order and pastoral calm existed in Lobel's manner of working. "When I illustrate, I have a system, and system is comfort. It makes me happy and secure."[43] One of the most accomplished and varied illustrators, Lobel often worked within limitations of color or production that others would have refused to accept. If there were no restrictions, he often set limitations for himself, as he felt that was how he did his best work.[44] External order clearly fostered creative expansion within. No matter what his project was at the time, Lobel worked, as friend and fellow artist James Marshall described, shopkeeper's hours, "working from nine till four, five days a week and [producing] wonderful imaginative stuff. . . . He wouldn't put pen to paper after five o'clock if he was paid a million dollars."[45] As he described it himself in his Harper & Row biographical release, Lobel's whole approach to writing was ordered, even though he often felt at a loss because he had no clear system as with illustrating:

> I supply myself with a not very intimidating notebook and an unassuming set of sharpened yellow pencils. I

find a quiet and comfortable corner of the house and I
begin. It can be a long and frustrating time for me. For
every good day when things are ripping along nicely,
there are two or three days when nothing whatsoever
happens—except that I chew the ends off a great many
of those yellow pencils. I've learned to persist and to be
patient, however, and eventually I arrive at a text that I
believe is finished enough to begin drawing the pictures
for. I still keep changing, or rather eliminating—for I try
to take out every word that does not really have to be
there. When it comes to the words of a picture book, less
is almost always very definitely more.[46]

Always one to write from his own behavior, Lobel frequently
extended his love of order to reductio ad absurdum. He often said
that "The Crocodile in the Bedroom" in *Fables* was based on his
own sense of order and extreme tidiness. The frontispiece illustration of the crocodile in the garden was one of the few original
works of his own that he kept in his apartment's primary rooms.
Order taken to extremes for humorous effect also occurs in
Grasshopper on the Road, the *Frog and Toad* books, and stories
he told on himself.

The well for much of his humor, it was Lobel's outwardly
ordered life and inwardly inspired manner of working that gave
his final years their fitting richness and dignity. Diagnosed
with a fatal illness (Acquired Immune Deficiency Syndrome) in
the spring of 1986, he initially tried to convince himself and others that perhaps it was the appropriate time to die. Then, accepting that there was nothing appropriate about dying so young and
at the height of one's career, Lobel simply (in *his* eyes) decided to
"approach it as his new job, something that he had to do as well
as he could."[47] He did it very well indeed, maintaining humor long
after others would have cursed and spit like Hildilid did at the
night. Family and friends along with home—the heart of his pastoral world—helped a great deal as did work itself as long as his
strength allowed. The vibrant pages of *The Devil and Mother
Crump* by Valerie Carey, *Tyrannosaurus Was a Beast* by Jack Pre-

lutsky, and his own dazzling *The Turnaround Wind* were all created as his life was ending.

Animals

Lobel's innate interest in a world that celebrated our inner common bonds rather than our external differences drew him to anthropomorphism as it did to the pastoral and humor. By writing of frogs, toads, mice, owls, and other animals, Lobel, like all fabulists, was really writing of people everywhere and of every color, class, and shape. Anthropomorphism was a vital ingredient in creating his pastoral world of freedom. These characters also allowed him to create versions of the pastoral archetype of child-adult or, as Lobel referred to them, "child-substitutes"[48] that were equally child and adult at once. Freed from human characteristics of age, anthropomorphic animals express the timelessness of Arcadia. Such characters can live alone as adults, share childlike interests, and experience emotional situations common to both without anyone feeling they are acting inappropriately. The use of child-substitutes or Arcadian animals also gave Lobel reason to exclude the traditional family that he had never had. "I feel more confident drawing animals. . . . But also, I don't like drawing people in contemporary clothes. There was a time when I was getting all these manuscripts about Mommy and Daddy in the kitchen. . . . I didn't have a Mommy and Daddy in the kitchen, and I don't know what Mommy and Daddy are like in the kitchen any more anyway."[49]

Lobel's connection with animals was far from restricted to a philosophical view of the pastoral. Like any child and perhaps especially like an only child, Lobel longed for pets. Childhood pets, however, were limited to a brief but all-too-successful experiment in breeding white mice and a failed attempt to adopt a live lobster he once found in the family refrigerator. With his own children Lobel shared many an afternoon watching animals at the Prospect Park Zoo in Brooklyn. He loved to recall that "The children were particularly fond of the vultures and the ice cream."[50]

At the same time that his fiction gave people the shapes of animals, Lobel gave his real animals the names of people. The Lobels shared their apartment with Seymour, their pet mouse, and after that Wilbur, a large turtle, renamed Wilbira upon producing eggs. There were also the career-changing frogs and toads the family befriended in Vermont, one of which Adrianne kept for some time.

Lobel placed both dogs and bats on his list of despised creatures, but avoided cats for fear of becoming too attached. It happened. Just as his children's frogs and toads and mice had sparked memorable books, daughter Adrianne's gift of a cat— named Orson after director Welles—sparked Lobel's joyful *Whiskers & Rhymes* and many illustrations in other books. After Orson's death Lobel acquired Alfred, the cover cat for *Whiskers & Rhymes,* who gave him great satisfaction.

Victorian Culture

One of Lobel's early and most treasured paintings features a Victorian girl, as Anita Lobel describes it, "in a stiff dress with a distant look in her eyes."[51] She is just the kind of child Lobel saw as waiting to be freed by Edward Lear's Victorian nonsense. Though Lobel never overtly refers to the Victorian culture in his narratives, the period's sensibilities and images are pervasive in his work. When blocked in his own creative work, he would often turn to his collection of children's books, "especially the old ones. Those Victorians seem to help at such times."[52] Edward Lear and the Victorian view of humor as pastoral holiday were particularly influential and / or kindred to Lobel's work. The constant duality of the Victorian world interested Lobel and was ultimately well suited to his pastoral voice. Just as Arcadia and Frog and Toad balance work and play, impulse and reason, innocence and experience, Victorian England balanced worldliness and provincialism, reform and reaction. For Victorians this balance culminated in a daily double life of a very ordered public surface and a very private personal life, a manner of living Lobel viewed as favorable.

Lobel was not alone in blending the Victorian and pastoral. The Victorians had done it themselves. Victorians in general showed a great interest in ancient Greece, and writers including Oscar Wilde and E. M. Forster often used the images of Theocritus' pastoral works as symbols for their own versions of Arcadia.[53]

The use of Victorian costumes and settings was natural for the folk rhymes Lobel began illustrating in the late seventies, but it also allowed him to maintain the distance that he desired from contemporary images and rigid roles. Dressed as Victorians, his characters give readers a world outside their own, a distant and quieter time in which they can temporarily rest. "Stiff," elegant Victorian clothing also adds to the humor and incongruity of behavior and appearance. "Polly Barlor, in the parlor" of *Whiskers & Rhymes* is not just an unruly child playing with her gum. She is a cat so proper she could be waiting to see Queen Victoria herself. The slovenly manners of Crane in "The Pelican and the Crane" and the spitball throwing of the family in "The Bad Kangaroo" (both in *Fables*) are given an immediate air of reductio ad absurdum when the characters are dressed in refined Victorian style. The comic havoc created by *The Turnaround Wind* is intensified because all who are turned around are out for a genteel Victorian walk and are as proper in attitude as in attire.

Frog and Toad and Owl do not wear Victorian clothing, but they live in cottages complete with flowers and lattice windows, the primary pastoral image of the Victorians.[54] A symbol of centuries gone unchanged, the cottage was viewed—as reflected in Lobel's books—as a place of solitude and simple living. It was an atmosphere Lobel surely absorbed during the family's holiday trip to the English countryside in the late sixties, and one that fed his intuitive work on the *Frog and Toad* books.

Nonsense

The element that ties all Lobel's pastoral notes together is his love of nonsense. Anthropomorphism is one of the first steps toward nonsense.[55] Nonsense is based in order turned inside out. Nonsense reached what many considered its zenith during England's Victorian era in the work of Edward Lear. And, as Elizabeth Sewell states in *The Field of Nonsense,* nonsense creates "its world from images of concrete everyday things,"[56] making it a perfect genre for Lobel's love of home and its accoutrements.

Lobel's childhood memories of Edward Lear's work were greatly revived when Anita gave him a three-volume set of Lear as an "inspired" gift for Christmas in 1975. Sir Edward Strachey, though describing Lear's nonsense in his introduction to the *Edward Lear Omnibus* (1943), could just as easily and accurately have been defining Lobel's sense of nonsense as pastoral. It was not, Strachey wrote, "a mere putting forward of incongruities and absurdities, but the bringing out [of] a new and deeper harmony of life in and through its contradiction."[57] Like Lear, Lobel's primary intent was to entertain or, in other words, to provide through humor a pastoral respite (albeit brief) from daily life's maze of rules and judgments. Basing his work on human foibles, Lobel was then able to reveal a good deal about the oneness of the human condition without falling into didacticism.

It is Lobel's intuitive awareness of nonsense as holiday or pastoral that gives his best work its distinctive quality. Understanding that both are based on amiable incongruities, Lobel was able to blend the seemingly incongruous forms of pastoral and nonsense into a gentle harmony.

Beyond their love of verse, absurd behavior, and love of cats and objects, Lobel and Lear shared a plot premise that is one of the ultimate topsy-turvy actions—taking the indoors out and the outdoors in. From his first text, *A Zoo for Mister Muster,* on, Lobel gently upset convention. Under his pen, animals leave the zoo. Pigs go to the city. Dishes go on a seaside holiday. Owl brings the winter inside, and rather than eating his cheese or keeping it stored, a cat in *Whiskers & Rhymes* wears it like a suit of clothes.

The reductio ad absurdum plot line of Dr. Seuss's *The 500 Hats of Bartholomew Cubbins* is the dominant element in Lobel's narrative grammar. In his words, he was "just the right age" when it was published in 1938; "It probably was one of the most decisive books of my life."[58] Though he did not elaborate about how or why, his own stories reveal a major connection. Frog and Toad don't just have a little trouble not eating cookies. Their story quickly spirals to an absurd level of tossing all the cookies to the birds. Owl isn't simply nervous about strange bumps at the foot of his bed, which are really his own feet. They soon come to dominate his life so completely that he gives "them" his bed and sleeps downstairs. The housefly that Grasshopper meets on the road (indeed, everyone but the worm) lives to absurd levels. The housefly has gone from sweeping up a single speck to trying to sweep the entire world. And the crocodile in the bedroom doesn't just prefer order to chaos: he clings so tightly to order that his life begins to slip away.

Reductio ad absurdum reflects Lobel's manner of seeing the world around him and the perspective that allowed him to see and celebrate nonsense. When taken to extremes, he saw human behavior, including his own, as inherently comic. A "morbidly tidy person,"[59] he did not simply straighten up the house, but once unknowingly, while on the cleaning prowl, tossed out Anita's finished sketches for a new picture book. A lucky search through a long row of garbage cans for familiar trash saved the drawings. In joking about his unremitting sense of neatness, Lobel frequently shared daughter Adrianne's joke that took his own behavior to reductio ad absurdum: she said he was so tidy that if she got up in the middle of the night, he'd have made her bed by the time she returned.

For Lobel's readers, reductio ad absurdum functions in the same manner that the pastoral functions for the writer, as "a vehicle for acceptance of the human condition."[60] Creating for the reader a literary dialectic experience, Lobel's stories have the distance of a fable. The reader moves from self-styled perfection (thesis), to absurd vicarious behavior (antithesis), to which the reader responds that he'd never go *that* far, and then halfway back (synthesis) to recognizing the core of that behavior in himself, and celebrating his humanness, warts and all.

"The Evening Meal," Lobel's little-known contribution to the *Scribner Anthology for Young People* (1976), manages to stretch four daily foibles to absurdity at once. Mrs. Goat gladly makes a big stew for her husband's meal, but it isn't enough. When he asks for more, she calmly tells him, "I have no more food to give you. You will just have to eat the plate." He does—*and* the cups and spoons as well. Mr. Goat keeps asking for more, and she keeps calmly suggesting he eat the table (he eats the table *and* the chair), then the walls (he eats the door and windows as well) until he begins to cry. Mrs. Goat asks if it is because he has eaten the plate, but he says no, as he does in regard to every object she mentions. Mr. Goat's eventual answer proves he is clearly living in the absurd, for he says the only reason he is crying is because he has a terrible ache in his stomach. At that moment Mrs. Goat, always calmly absurd, leaps into guilt squared and shouts:

> Oh, my dear husband.
> I'm so sorry, it is all my fault.
> You are crying because you have
> a terrible ache in your stomach
> because I must have put
> too many onions in the stew![61]

Within just a few words Lobel reveals gluttony, self-centeredness, eagerness to please, and readiness to accept guilt as the ridiculous and self-mocking actions they are, yet we laugh as we look in the mirror. As John Donovan wrote in 1976, "Lobel sees the light and shares it."[62] The source of Lobel's illumination was another form of light—laughter, the song of unity and triumph.[63]

As is true of all good friendships, the books and stories Lobel read and created nourished one another. By keeping the child within him alive, they gave him an adulthood he enjoyed, a balance best represented by his beloved gorilla suit. After years of wishing for just such a suit, Adrianne made him one for Christmas, complete with realistic head. Lobel loved it and wore it in the opening frames of the filmstrip Random House produced about him for their series *Meet the Newbery Author*.[64] His delight and sense of the playfully absurd, however, went far beyond the safe bounds of a filmstrip for children. On occasion, he would put it on for sheer pleasure, walk around his Brooklyn neighborhood, and the suit itself became a kind of Arcadia.

In receiving the George G. Stone Award from Claremont College in 1978 for his *Frog and Toad* series, Lobel closed his remarks with the following: "to be making books for children allows me the freedom and pleasures of being adult, and at the same time, I can always partake in a kind of childlike wonderment, and I guess walking about in a gorilla suit can certainly be put into the category of childlike wonderment. To be making books for children is to be in a sort of state of grace."[65]

Constantly re-creating it, Lobel never had to leave Arcadia. Quite fittingly, his ashes now rest in the garden of a friend.

2

Performing the Words of Others

I like to work with other people's manuscripts: it
gives my imagination a chance to stretch in different
ways.[1]

In the world of the picture book where stars are made, medals
won, and special effects all too often overshadow the complex
basics of good book design, Arnold Lobel became an illustrator's
illustrator. As Maurice Sendak wrote in *Publishers Weekly*'s "Arnold Lobel Remembered," "There was no pretentiousness, no
hokum, no ego-schticking to Arnold's work. There was a clarity
that could be enjoyed on the simplest level, but if you had a more
sophisticated sensibility, you saw how dense his work really was.
That simplicity, that beguiling surface, is the quintessential ingredient that makes a great artist."[2] In addition to the twenty-
eight titles he wrote and illustrated himself, Lobel also illustrated
over seventy books by other writers. To be sure, such a large number of books range in quality of text, and not all of them represent
Lobel's best work. What is most impressive is the variety. Best
known for the early reader, he also illustrated novels (*Witch on
the Corner* [1966] and *Master of Miracle* [1971]), nonfiction (*Dinosaur Time* [1974] and *The Microscope* [1984]), poetry (*Merry
Merry FIBruary* [1977] and *The Headless Horseman Rides To-*

night [1980]), what might best be called activity books (*Holiday Dictionary; With 90 Religious Objects to Color and 84 Full-Page Color Perforated Religious Objects Stamps* [1958]), and a quartet of preschool board books including *Where's the Cat?* (1987).

Having written some of the best and most lasting stories of his generation, Lobel enjoyed illustrating the writing of others throughout his career. He was, as he often called himself, a "journeyman illustrator,"[3] in the same way Sir John Gielgud referred to himself as a journeyman actor. Both were more interested in the quality of their work than in the size of their roles. They knew a supporting role well done was as vital to the whole as a prima donna's solo.

Lobel's first illustrative work in books for children was for Ktav Publishing House in New York. All were nonfiction on Jewish holidays and customs. For at least three (*My First Book of Prayers* by Edythe Scharfstein [1958], *Book of Chanukah: Poems, Riddles, Stories, Songs and Things to Do* by Edythe Scharfstein [1959], and *Holidays are Nice: Around the Year with the Jewish Child* by Robert Garvey [1960]) Lobel is credited as co-illustrator with Ezekiel Schloss. Ktav editor Bernard Scharfstein believes that the final title is the "most important of Arnold's illustrations" done for Ktav and "the beginning of the technique and style he developed and which made him a great illustrator of children's books."[4] Echoes of the stylized faces and cross-hatching can be found in many of Lobel's books of the sixties.

While his work for Ktav was a solid first step, Lobel's acceptance by Harper & Row was a significant leap. As a fledgling book illustrator, he could not have had a better training ground than the then-new "I Can Read" genre. Nor could the "I Can Read" authors have been paired with a new talent more suited to the genre's need for endless versatility within limitations. Beyond his illustration and design skills and preference for working within limitations, Lobel's love of reading as an experience made him a natural match for the growing literary genre. By the time he created the first volume of his famous *Frog and Toad* series in 1970, he had illustrated sixteen early readers including two of his own writing. The thirty early reader books Lobel illustrated in his career offer a rich overview of both his growth as an artist and his sensitivity to the texts.

Lobel's first illustrative assignment with Harper & Row and first "I Can Read" manuscript was Fred Phleger's *Red Tag Comes Back* (1961). Illustrated in pen and ink with preseparated wash, it was, to quote Lobel, "64 [*sic*] pages of pictures of salmon swimming upstream. They wouldn't have dreamed of giving it to an artist who had any kind of reputation. But I did it and once I had my foot in the door and knew a few people, I was able to continue."[5] His retrospective assessment may be true in many ways, but the atmosphere then surrounding the new genre is equally telling. Though both Dr. Seuss's *Cat in the Hat* and the *Little Bear* books by Minarik and Sendak, now viewed as classics, had already been published, the genre was hungry for new talent. Most well-established writers and illustrators were rejecting any connection with the new form, then seen by many as merely a gussied-up basal reader. Susan Hirschman, then Ursula Nordstrom's assistant editor at Harper, recalls that Lobel's portfolio showed he could illustrate anything.[6] Within a short span of time, he was.

Red Tag Comes Back may lack finesse in the execution of preseparated washes, but its design is energetic and varied. Lobel shares the quiet wooded moments as clearly as he does the sweeping dangers of the sea and of being caught. Twenty-seven years later this book remains in print, and author Phleger, a professor of oceanography, feels Lobel's illustrations give "an excellent feeling for the environments and the activities."[7]

Lobel's illustrations just two years later for Millicent Selsam's *Greg's Microscope* (1963), a "Science I Can Read" book, demonstrate his range of tone, texture, and visual evocation. Lobel used pencil drawings as his base with limited preseparated color created by both pencil and wash. It is a family story (one of the few human families he ever worked on), and Lobel's images are warm and tactile. His illustrations not only evoke the warmth of the family, but their textures also draw in the reader's eye for a closer look, just as Greg does with his microscope, seeing everyday objects anew.

Done in muted blue, yellow, and green, Lobel's illustrations are a blend of the nuclear family he did not have as a child and the close family he was then enjoying with his wife and two young children. The father genuinely listens when young Greg talks and is interested in what Greg feels and sees. This is, of course, a part of Selsam's text, but Lobel makes it realized action through the tone and content of his images. His initial illustrations of Greg and his father show them sharing time together as they work in the garden. Greg's mother is equally warm and attentive. Done in the sharp ink lines and hatching he used for Mildred Myrick's *Secret Three* of the same year or in the bold cartoon line and colors of Nathaniel Benchley's *Red Fox and His Canoe* (1964), the familial warmth of *Greg's Microscope* would have easily dissolved.

Lobel was paired with Benchley for four "I Can Read" books. Two of them, *Oscar Otter* (1966) and *Sam the Minuteman* (1969), demonstrate once again Lobel's sensitivity to tone of story. Illustrations for *Oscar Otter* are quick-lined with minimal shading and sparse backgrounds. Oscar's smirk on the title page sums up Lobel's understanding of his character. Such a proud, cocky creature is destined to fall. An extension of Benchley's broad comic action, Lobel's pen-and-ink line is as active as Oscar's adventure. Between the first and final illustrations featuring Oscar's home pond, there isn't a single quiet moment or static image in the book.

In contrast, Lobel's illustrations for *Sam the Minuteman* (a stronger and more satisfying text) are appropriately everything his work in *Oscar Otter* is not. A family story set during the early days of the American Revolution, the entire book evokes a sense of old pewter and framed memories. Lobel builds his images by chiaroscuro, adding pencil hatching and at times a thin ink line to heighten shape. An olive wash is used selectively to highlight the colonialists and the land and homes they were fighting to free. Red appears only in the coats of the British soldiers and in the blood they draw from Sam's young friend during battle.

Through both design and gesture, Lobel reveals small family dramas as well as the battling troops. The tactile sense of pewter not only evokes the Revolutionary period, but also, with its quiet shadows, the hush of waiting for the troops to arrive. Lobel's "staging" of scenes reveals the conflicting emotions war brings. When young Sam comes down the stairs as the church bells call their warning, the reader sees not only Sam's curiosity, but his father's eager and firm-faced preparations and his mother's deep concern. Most dramatic of all is a series of three illustrations (pages 34–39), each one adding tension to the one before it. Beginning the sequence on page 34, Lobel places the colonialists behind a stone fence and cramped in the lower left-hand corner of a vertical frame. The empty road slopes down the hill and dominates the page. It is clear even without Benchley's text that the huddled colonialists are waiting with caution for trouble. A turn of the page finds the same image suddenly filled with red-coated soldiers marching closer and closer, their ranks so close they create another wall. The colonialists remain huddled in the corner not daring to move. Following these two vertical images with most of the space towering over the colonialists, Lobel's next illustration is a horizontal image that fills the top half of the two-page spread. A wide or panoramic shot, the scene is made dramatic by its content and design. It is as if Lobel's cinematic camera begins crouched with the colonialists, sharing their physical and visual point of view, and then dollies back and to the left revealing, as it is revealed to the colonialists, the true magnitude of the situation. The red-coated soldiers dominate as they march in a straight line like a wall across the left three-quarters of the image. The colonialists remain clustered behind their stone wall and tucked in the lower right-hand corner. On the other side of the British troops are the land and homes for which they are fighting. Between themselves and the bright red-coated soliders are the graves of others. Every element adds to the tension of the battle soon to begin.

In this story of battles Lobel consistently recalls the relationships of those involved. While Benchley's concluding text focuses on Sam, Lobel's illustration again depicts the emotional burden and helplessness of wives and mothers during war. As Sam goes upstairs to bed, his dog playfully follows. While it has been a day that has changed him in many ways, Sam is still a child. Behind the stairs are his parents, embracing one another. It is clear that they know they could have lost one another again, and while today was lucky, the next battle may be different.

In the early seventies, as Lobel was working on his soon-to-be-famous *Frog and Toad* volumes, he was also creating some of the best illustrations in the genre for texts by others. After ten years of working within the "I Can Read" genre, he was clearly as at home with the form as a romantic writer is with the sonnet. Rather than attempting to graft on formats of larger picture books, he continued to expand within the form's limitations.

Like the early reader sentences, Lobel's illustrations are complete, yet brief. There is always breath around them, just as there is breathing space around the text itself. His frequent framing or partial framing of images, while in part decoration, greatly contributes to the sense of order and safety of the book. Such illustrations offer guidance to the new reader's eye just as do the large typeface and short lines. The values of color and the darkness of images were also significant concerns to Lobel. As he stated in the mid-seventies, "You learn that if the color gets too strong for those little books . . . and that big type . . . it looks lousy. And I've done it. In my early years I used to do bright colors in those things and I really wasn't happy with them, so I gradually got muter and muter and became more pleased with the aesthetic result."[8] From beginning to end Lobel gave the "I Can Read" books he illustrated a tone of inner calmness, intimacy, and manageability— the oasis he knew reading could be.

Robert Morris's *Seahorse* (1972) and Cynthia Jameson's *The Clay Pot Boy* (1973) remain two of the best-illustrated early reader books ever done. Each was cited in its respective year for outstanding design by the Children's Book Council and included in their Children's Book Showcase. Both are also excellent examples of Lobel's cinematic use of frames.

Set entirely under water, *Seahorse*'s illustrations almost require frames as a means of containing the ocean. Without framing, images of water would just suddenly stop in mid-flow. Lobel's choice of a thin framing line also creates the sense of an aquarium which would allow the reader to view such sea life. Using pencil drawings and pencil overlays printed in three colors, Lobel creates both the translucence and the varying sense of depth of water. Particularly effective are his tight, horizontal, light pencil lines that interweave with each illustration. The uneven value of the lines contributes to the sense of underwater undulation.

The illustrations for *Seahorse* could easily be brought to life as a science film. Lobel follows Morris's lead in the text and sets broad scenes, moves closer to share more detailed information, then closer still for dramatic close-ups of action all but invisible to the naked eye. As he frequently did when illustrating fictional texts, Lobel frames the entire manuscript with beginning and concluding images of home. Here it is the sea, in the beginning a sea storm and, after the seahorse journey through birth, a calm moonlit bay.

Cynthia Jameson's adaptation of a Russian tale entitled *The Clay Pot Boy* is also a fine example of Lobel's dynamic use of framing. Again he begins and ends the narrative with the image of home, this time using the same image twice. Small and oval in shape, the illustration of the couple posed in front of their home resembles an old miniature painting or daguerreotype. These framing illustrations imply that the narrative once happened to people known by others and is a story now being remembered and retold. The frontispiece illustration adds to this illusion for it depicts not the couple of the story, but a neighboring mother and son watching the clay pot boy stomp through their land. Having seen it happen, they are naturally eager to pass the story on, which is exactly what the following pages do.

Every page, whether containing text or illustration, is thinly framed near trim size, and images are frequently framed again within that frame, acting much like a zoom lens to intensify perspective and drama. After beginning with the miniature wide-shot image of the couple in front of their home, Lobel's camera moves closer, filling the doublespread screen with the couple to establish their roles in the story. The succeeding image or "shot" focuses on the just-completed clay pot boy. He stands in the center of the framed image with the sun beaming in through the window behind him. The large shadow he casts toward the reader is a subtle forewarning of his oncoming change in size. The loving couple (and unlucky proud parents) stand one to each side. From this point onward Lobel alternates doublespread images in pen and ink with single-page images in pen and ink with gray and gold wash—with a few exceptions. Doublespreads function as long shots and establish a change in setting, while single-page images are used as close-ups at the peak moment of action. Size of image on single-page illustrations also varies; the smaller or tighter the shot, the greater the impending danger. These alternating image dimensions add drama to the clay pot boy's increasing size and villainy. The degree to which he fills the framed space informs the reader of his current size as certainly as it shows his relationship to other objects.

As with *Seahorse,* a representative cycle best demonstrates Lobel's talent. On page 43 the clay pot boy is swallowing a wooden barn after having already consumed ten tubs of milk, five baskets of bread, the old lady and her spinning wheel, the old man and his walking stick, the bull, the woodchopper with his ax, the farmer with his hoe, the farmer's wife with her rake, the crowing rooster, and the hen sitting on an egg. By this point he is gigantic, and his act of eating the barn fills the page. But he gets still larger on the following doublespread. Now he is peeking out from behind a hill with his next meal—a goat—in the foreground. From there one turns the page to a close-up that shows both the comparable size of the two characters and the certainty of the goat's demise. The use of triple framing, rather than merely a single small static image, actively draws in the reader's eye as in a zoom shot. Beginning with the doublespread trim size, Lobel pulls the reader's eye in to the single-page outer frame and then in still closer to the smaller framed image (a quarter of the page in size) of the clay pot boy's gaping mouth. Having fixed the visual danger in the reader's mind, Lobel then pulls back to set up the action—the goat on the hilltop and the clay pot boy waiting at the bottom with mouth open wide. With the turn of the page and a quick zoom shot (but appropriately not as tight as the previous one), the goat jumps and strikes the clay pot boy. The image is in mid-crash and the broken pieces of clay are exploding out of the frame that held the clay pot boy. This time, rather than contributing to the closure of an image, Lobel's frame creates energy because its order is broken. An exploding clay pot boy is simply too big to be contained.

Depth of Field

As Lobel's career evolved and his work matured from his early expectations about what a picture book should be to his own realization of what a picture book could be, his illustrations developed a greater visual depth of field. As he told Lucy Rollin in *Children's Literature in Education*, "In my early work, like *Mister Muster,* the whole style was influenced by watching television over the heads of my children."[9] Once his children were too tall to see over and no longer watching cartoons, Lobel, as he states later in the same interview, "had more time to be introspective and study the work of other artists that I liked."[10] Rembrandt, for example, was a direct influence on Lobel while he was illustrating *The Microscope* by Maxine Kumin.

His *A Zoo for Mister Muster* and *Lucille,* as well as *The Quarreling Book* by Charlotte Zolotow, are visual cousins of the television cartoon. Primarily created by outline, the characters in these books live most of their narrative lives on a single vertical plane near the surface of the paper. Depth or horizon line is included only when needed to transport the characters, and then it is as minimal in style as are the characters themselves. These visual simplicities are appropriate for these texts. *The Quarreling Book,* for example, could have easily become too self-conscious and didactic if the illustrations had been more realistic. Lobel's airy cartoon style succeeds in much the same way as animals do in fables. It is just far enough removed from the child's tangible world to avoid pointing a finger, yet close enough for the child to recognize the setting, situation, emotions, and eventually himself.

A Zoo for Mister Muster and its companion volume, *A Holiday for Mister Muster* (1964), also succeed because of their flatter cartoon style. Both narratives are absurd fantasies. In a cartoon everything is possible and hence believable. If Lobel had illustrated them in a more realistic style, the lightness of their humor would have been squelched. Had he used a more intricate style, their spontaneity—the core of absurdity and nonsense—could have been stilled as it was with *The Four Little Children Who Went Around the World.*

Lobel's illustrations for books of the mid-sixties, such as Miriam Young's *Miss Suzy* (1964) and Andrea DiNoto's *Star Thief* (1967), began having fuller and more detailed settings with deeper backgrounds and horizon lines. A greater sense of depth or roundedness in characters also began to appear through his use of crosshatching (*Let's Get Turtles* [1965]), cross-hatching and wash (*The Four Little Children Who Went Around the World* [1968]), and chiaroscuro by pencil rubbing (*The Terrible Tiger* and *Sam the Minuteman,* both of 1969). Following his philosophy of using anything needed to make an illustration the best it could be and at the same time developing greater trust in his instincts, Lobel began to use varied combinations of these techniques as well as others. Self-doubt and working to compensate for a visual problem also contributed to the growth in his work. "I don't think my work would have grown an inch if I had not always been dissatisfied and filled with self-doubt. I feel my work is very flat. . . . Depth and form are difficult because I have no depth perception. I don't have bifocal vision. The image is totally suppressed on one of my eyes."[11]

The Microscope by Maxine Kumin and his own *Whiskers & Rhymes,* both published in 1985, exist deep into the paper. Using only pen and ink, Lobel's cross-hatching in *The Microscope* is so complex and minute that it creates the continuous shading of chiaroscuro. The playful verses of *Whiskers & Rhymes* are illustrated with such depth through line and color that Donnarae MacCann and Olga Richard referred to the "strong sculptural quality" of the pictures, which suggest "objects a child could pick up and arrange in different settings."[12]

Color and Line

Throughout his career Lobel carefully chose limited color or black and white when he felt it best suited the text. When he did use full color it was not simply because it was easier or demonstrated his stature, but because it was a vital element of his illustrative performance.

His first full book to be done in watercolor was *Miss Suzy's Easter Surprise* (1972). Miriam Young's tale of an anthropomorphic squirrel family is naturally filled with spring flower colors. Lobel's brushwork and pencil highlights give the fantasy the lightness and translucence it needs to be believed. Two following watercolor works, *Miss Suzy's Birthday* by Young (1974) and *Merry Merry FIBruary* by Doris Orgel (1977), were selected in their respective years by the *New York Times Book Review* as Best Illustrated Children's Books of the Year.

When he began illustrating more often in watercolor, Lobel worked with the same symbiosis to text that marks his limited color illustrations in the "I Can Read" volumes. *Gregory Griggs* (1978), *Fables* (1980), *Whiskers & Rhymes* (1985), *A Three Hat Day* by Laura Geringer (1985), *The Random House Book of Mother Goose* (1986), and *Tyrannosaurus was a Beast* by Jack Prelutsky (1988) are all primarily watercolor but very different from one another. *Gregory Griggs* is pastel in palette with characters set against the white page or the palest of skies. *Fables* is more "finished" or Victorian in nature. Colors are darker and deeper with no bare paper exposed. Most forms are delineated by line, and all characters are given complete settings. The illustrations for *Fables* are at once rich in texture and thoroughly contained. His illustrations for *Tyrannosaurus Was a Beast,* while framed, are filled with tropical light and as light in tone and brush stroke as those in *Fables* are deep and restrained.

As befits the wide range and number of rhymes in his *Mother Goose,* Lobel's illustrations include all he had learned of illustration. Alison Lurie wrote in the *New York Times Book Review* that his "lively, colorful, comical drawings almost burst from the page."[13] The illustration for "Hush, little baby" is hushed in color and shading, soft in line, and safely contained by a thin double frame. In contrast, "There was an old woman who lived in a shoe" is dark and thick in colors that spill over one another, dark and frenetic in line, and barely contained by its entire doublespread. "Gray Goose and gander" is in light-filled pastel and is as quiet in tone as the good king's daughter's ride in the sky. However, "Jack Sprat could eat no fat" is as extreme and brazen in color as his wife's appetite and as ragged in shading as her manners.

Fellow author-artist James Marshall believed Lobel to be "without doubt, one of the very finest watercolorists who ever lived"[14] and praised his palette as one of the "most exuberant and original"[15] in books. Lobel learned from English watercolorists and then as with every form and media he studied, expanded what he learned in ways that became his and his alone.

Theater and Film

Beginning with his childhood production of plays in the cellar for friends Lobel was familiar with theatrical space. Not only was it a solid influence on his early illustrations, but the primary way in which he described his work as an illustrator. When asked if he shared his early drafts with children, he wrote, "I never try my ideas out on children—they should see the finished performance, not the rehearsal."[16]

Lobel's illustrations for two books by Charlotte Zolotow demonstrate his sense of theater. While it does use several different settings, *The Quarreling Book* is primarily illustrated with vignettes of action and little depth of field. It is clearly the theater's world of acknowledged pretending rather than film's pretense of reality. All scenes are viewed from the same perspective, and visual emphasis remains on character action rather than setting.

Lobel's sense of theater is more direct in Zolotow's *Someday*. The cover presents the child narrator dancing on a stage, and the visual sense of a school play persists throughout most of the book. Backgrounds are simple (more sets than reality), almost all characters and action are depicted on the same horizon line, and, for the most part, all action is viewed from the same perspective. The reader is clearly given the position of a member of a theater audience.

As Lobel began to prefer film over theater, both his books and metaphors changed to reflect the film world. "In a book, you are using pictures in a narrative way," he stated in the early eighties, "and the turning of the page is like a cut in a movie. If a movie is well done and you're caught up in it, even if you know the plot backwards and forwards, you're still pulled along by a rhythm. Alfred Hitchcock movies are a good example. And in children's books, the pictures have a rhythm, from large to small, for instance. And sometimes really sequential pictures work, but I wouldn't force that on something that I didn't think called for it."[17]

Hitchcock and film in general also served as sources of instruction. "I think I learned more about illustrating children's books from movies than from any other art form: the selection of images, the narrative, and the way of showing things. . . . [Hitchcock] has been one of my mentors in terms of telling a story that is entertaining and yet has a whole other side."[18]

Lobel's performance of Edward Lear's "The Story of the Four Little Children Who Went Round the World" (on which he remembered working very hard)[19] is his first major use of varying visual perspectives. Lobel's initial images are calm and direct, as is the beginning of Lear's story, but his illustrations soon accelerate in design and variety of perspective as the children's adventures do. With *The Four Little Children Who Went Around the World* (he altered the title) Lobel began to use full frontal close-ups, long parting shots, detailed close-ups, high-angle shots, and varying depths of field. There is no way the reader can experience the illustrations as if sitting in a theater seat. Just as the text is an adventure around the world to nonhuman places, Lobel's illustrations are an adventure of traveling through nonhuman perspectives.

Lear's verse tale *The New Vestments* (1970) was Lobel's next move toward film. As with *The Comic Adventures of Old Mother Hubbard* each page of illustration is framed, but here the frames function more as roving windows on outdoor action than as separate stage scenes. *The New Vestments* is a tale of great physical action, and Lobel reaches deep into the page using many horizontal planes. Sets, direction and movement, and horizon lines are constantly changing, which is impossible in the theater. Lobel's use of varying paths of visual movement and perspective creates an effect resembling the edited camera shots of a film sequence. At times characters are right at the reader's feet, at other times they're ten feet away, and at still other times the reader views the action as if from a blimp or steeple tower. The designs of pages 10–29 are particularly effective in evoking the panic and confusion the old man of Tess feels as he is attacked from all sides. For the reader, the consuming of the old man's new vestments is a visceral, frenetic event.

Framing

Lobel created a sense of cinematic rhythm in both Cheli Ryan's *Hildilid's Night* (1971) and Anne Rose's *As Right as Right Can Be* (1976) by using varying sizes of framed images that play against both the page as initial frame and against one another. If one views the size of his framed images as the depth and length of a musical note, his illustrations become the perfect background rhythm for each story's film score. The size of frame, particularly horizontal length, also corresponds with the length of a film cut. The slower and / or calmer the scene the longer the piece of film before cutting to another. The faster or more frantic the scene the shorter the pieces of film as they quickly cut from one to another.

Lobel begins *Hildilid's Night* with a small tight shot of a lantern—the object Hildilid values most. The title page, a two-page spread, is dominated, as is Hildilid, by a massive black night sky. This is followed by a smaller framed image of her peeking out from behind her curtains. The reader sees only her face and the window. By the time the story begins with a single-page illustration that depicts Hildilid, her house, and the surrounding area the reader already knows (as with film during opening credits)

Hildilid's relationship with the night. Early scenes or illustrations that continue to establish her character and fears of the dark are larger and longer, creating a relaxed pace. As Hildilid begins to attack the night, however, her actions become more vigorous. Lobel's framed images become smaller, and he quickens the story's pace by placing more than one framed image per page. Emotional length of scenes is linked with the physical length of framed images. The boiling of a cauldron requires and is given more time than a snip of the shears or a singe with a candle.

As Hildilid's despair grows into a frenzy, Lobel speeds up his framed images by reducing their size and increasing their proximity and number per page. Then, when in utter disgust Hildilid stops all her fighting and spits at the night, Lobel switches back to a nearly full-sized single-page image, matching the magnitude of the action and the stillness and length of the scene. It is the scene before both Hildilid and her story begin their denouement. Lobel's succeeding image of her after losing the battle is even larger, filling two-thirds of the doublespread. Hildilid is walking angrily out of the lower left-hand corner as the immense night stretches up and to the right, covering miles and miles of farmland and homes. The final illustration is a slightly smaller version of the opening image depicting her home, but with two changes. This time Hildilid is inside her house asleep, and the warm golden sun colors everything.

With *Hildilid's Night* Lobel also uses what exists outside the frame to maximum effect. Each pen-and-ink drawing is framed by an eighth inch of white, then framed by an ink line. Outside this is the rest of the white page. Surrounded by white, the blackness of Hildilid's dreaded night becomes even blacker by contrast. The out-of-frame space is for the most part larger than the illustration and so also contributes to the reader's sense of Hildilid's isolation. Few picture books have used the actual page and its innate emptiness to such powerful effect. Rather than simply containing the story, Lobel uses the book's physicality as an active medium in telling the story.

In *As Right as Right Can Be* Lobel, with a few appropriate exceptions, uses only two sizes of framed images. And, as in *Hildi-*

lid's Night, the varying sizes are consistent with the narrative's rhythm. The story is one of spiraling wish and action, and Lobel begins each doublespread with a thin vertical framed image on the far left side of the left-hand page. Related text is to its right. These left-hand pages of text and image present the character as he stops to make a wish. The framed image on the right-hand page, illustrating the granted wish, is two and one half times wider than that of the wish while the same height. This rhythm of stop–then action continues until the character, Ron Ronson, is satisfied.

Lobel's rhythmic pattern changes for the first time when Ron reaches home and is rejected by his wife who no longer recognizes him. At this point the couple, the story, and Lobel's design all find a new balance. Rona Ronson gets new clothes to match those of her husband, and for the first time the framed images on left- and right-hand pages are equal in dimension. Their sense of balance and satisfaction, however, is short-lived. Their wishes and Lobel's wish-action rhythm begin again and continue until the many angry creditors carry off all the Ronsons' new possessions. With this scene Lobel effectively breaks his pattern—the pattern of their life is being destroyed—and uses two horizontal images in the bottom half of both pages to depict the parade of their possessions being carried away.

With all their new possessions gone, Ron and Rona Ronson are once again equal and back to their old selves. And once again Lobel has balanced his pages with two smaller vertical images placed at the far left and right sides of the doublespread. After one last sequence of wish-action, the Ronsons are back in their poor old home where things are as right as right can be. Lobel has placed them in rocking chairs in the middle of a single large image on the right-hand page. After a narrative of continual change this final image is Lobel's final full chord that confirms the story's end by its breadth and quiet established by the lack of any action.

Lobel's use of framing is not confined to creating a sense of theater or cinema. His later work illustrating the mock-horrific poetry of Jack Prelutsky and his own *Fables* and *Pigericks* turned frames into the private chambers he admired in Edward Lear's work. "Each drawing and poem," as he described his edition of Lear, "is on a right-hand page facing a blank page on the left. Thus each episode has a chamber of its own, so to speak, no crowding."[20]

There could scarcely be a better term than *chamber* to describe Lobel's framed images for Prelutsky's *Nightmares: Poems to Trouble Your Sleep* (1976) and *The Headless Horseman Rides Tonight* (1980). Since most of the poems have only one illustration rather than a sequence, Lobel's use of frames in these books gives each image an honored chamber of its own. Dominating the pages on which they appear, the images readily evoke the uncertainty of dark corners and the silence just before a scream. Each pen-and-ink illustration is framed by an inch of white and seems as isolated as the doomed or evil characters depicted. Lobel's design and illustration create safely disturbing chambers of horrors like the chamber of darkness he experienced while watching horror movies as a child.[21]

Such framed chambers, however, need not always be macabre. As Lear in some editions of his limericks and Lobel in his *Fables* and *Book of Pigericks* show, framed page-size illustrations can also be familiar parlor-chambers in which comic behavior can be observed and safely revealed. Lobel's multiple framing in both *Fables* and *Pigericks* creates a sense of intimacy by enclosing an expansive image, and at the same time it creates the illusion of greater depth.

Whether macabre or familiar, such chambers are appropriate for the genre of poetry. Containing far less plot or characterization than narratives designed for multiple pages, short poems (and fables, too) are truly best illustrated by single images. Solitary illustrations allow the visuals to concentrate on the text's dominant elements of tone and atmosphere and highlight what is usually the text's one key action. For an illustrator to expand a nonnarrative poem or fable into a sequence of images is likely to create a case of rewriting through "filler" details and a shift in the text's meaning. Or, at best, it may stretch it to a weakening thinness.

From *The Headless Horseman Rides Tonight* by Jack Prelutsky, illustrated by
Arnold Lobel. Illustrations © 1980 by Arnold Lobel. Reprinted by permission
of Greenwillow Books (a Division of William Morrow & Company, Inc.), p. 19.
Photographed from the artist's original pen and ink drawing: 16.2 cm × 12.4
cm.

The Artist as Actor

Just as Lobel used the theater and cinema as metaphors for picture books, he compared the role of an illustrator with that of an actor. "A good illustrator," he states in *Illustrators of Children's Books: 1957–1966,* "should have a repertory of styles at his command—like an actor switching from role to role."[22] While many of the texts he illustrated might have been successfully illustrated by others, Lobel's interpretation or performance is so complete that it is difficult to imagine that story in any other form. *A Zoo for Mister Muster* rings as true with its controlled and tailored line, which matches the character's orderly life, as do Lobel's wildly kinetic illustrations of Mother Goose characters whom he viewed as "bawdy and naughty."[23] The angry and flailing world of *Hildilid's Night* is brought to life through Lobel's short emphatic line. Arranged to build form and depth, his lines each remain in isolation (as does Hildilid) with no cross-hatching to interweave or soften areas. In direct contrast, *Someday*'s line is as muted and airy as the narrator's daydreams. And in contrast to all is Valerie Scho Carey's *The Devil and Mother Crump* (1987). Lobel's performance of this tale about battles between the devil and a woman even meaner than the devil uses ink line only to highlight a moody chiaroscuro world just waiting to engulf its victims. As ominous as its black is, *The Devil and Mother Crump* remains a boisterous comedy through Lobel's palette of fire-bright gold, green, red, and blue that are as archetypal in value as the story's elements. As always, the range of color Lobel used was an extension of the text. To color his black-and-white or limited color illustrations would be as much a lessening of quality as to reduce his watercolors to black and white.

Just as he did with texts in his highly ordered literary forms (verse, "I Can Read," and fable) Lobel created visual richness within restrictions. In his hands less almost always became more. "Sometimes limitations are an asset," he told illustration professor Nancy Hands. "If I don't have limitations, I make some myself, such as size and color. Becoming a professional is knowing what is most comfortable for you."[24] Limited color was used in early readers as a way of keeping cost down, but as discussed above, Lobel also saw aesthetic reasons.

As Right as Right Can Be is another example of Lobel creating more with less. It is successful because its images have a naive flatness of both shape and color. Though Anne Rose's text gives no geographical or historical setting, Lobel places it in early America. The flatness of shape and style of clothing are reminiscent of colonial or less sophisticated painting. Lobel's broken ink line resembles stitchery, quite appropriate for characters living in darned clothes while dreaming of riches. To have illustrated *As Right as Right Can Be* in the rich full-bodied style of *Whiskers & Rhymes* or the detailed lines of *Nightmares: Poems to Trouble Your Sleep* would have been like having a diva in full opera regalia sing "I Know an Old Lady Who Swallowed a Fly."

Lobel's two "dinosaur performances" illustrate his sensitivity to the voice and form of a text and his talent in extending both elements through line and color. His dinosaurs for Peggy Parish's *Dinosaur Time* (1974) are as calm, ordered, and contained as the "I Can Read" format. It is a book of direct information, and Lobel presents his dinosaurs in a low-key but scholarly fashion through controlled pen-and-ink drawings with limited wash. They are dinosaurs of science. The same dinosaurs are given new lives in his illustrations for *Tyrannosaurus Was a Beast* (1988). Prelutsky's text shares scientific information, but it does so through rollicking verse. Here, Lobel's dinosaurs have the barest touch of anthropomorphism and often glance into the reader's world. Some, like the Ankylosaurus, stare in warning, while others, like the Triceratops, seem startled that a human is watching his nonhuman world. The Tyrannosaurus on the cover stands grinning like a misbehaving ten-year-old who is enjoying his wickedness. Just as Prelutsky's words slide together in rhyme and bounce off one another so do Lobel's lines and colors. Mottled and seeming to reflect off one another, they move with the playfulness of the verses. Every image shares the warm, breezy interplay of colors on a tropical forest afternoon. And, like Prelutsky's verses, Lobel's line never stops moving; it is forever taking an eye-catching turn.

In a world of cloned and derivative art Lobel remained distinct,

evolving, and true to his work. It is this very uniqueness and evo-
lution that has prevented others from copying his style. Like the
best of contemporary actors such as Robert DeNiro, Meryl Streep,
and William Hurt, each new performance, each new role is so distinct and individual there is nothing to impersonate in Lobel's
performance except growth and change.

Honoring the Reader

Pastoral images of home and garden that symbolize Lobel's pleasure in reading appear throughout his illustrative work. What is
less obvious is his honoring of his readers and the act of reading.
At the same time as they provide decorative design and direction,
his frames also provide windows that acknowledge the coexistence of the reader's world and the storyworld. The books by another writer which most clearly show Lobel's sense of parallel
worlds and reading time are Jack Prelutsky's two volumes of
mock-horrific verse.

A skeleton on the cover of *Nightmares* . . . is about to hand the
reader a rose. On the dedication page a rose (the rose the skeleton
gave the reader?) is in a vase and beginning to wilt. Twelve verses
later the reader turns the last page and sees the same rose, or
rather its remains, for it has completely wilted and lost its petals
as he read. *The Headless Horseman Rides Tonight* literally illustrates the interweaving of actual and fictional worlds through
reading. The title page features a small framed image of a "darkling elf" sitting in the top of a tree. Consciously or not, the image
registers in the reader's mind. A verse near the center of the book
is about the same creatures now identified as "darkling elves."
Their verse only describes their readiness to attack. Lobel's accompanying image shows them waiting in the top of a tree, waiting to jump down on someone reading in the shade of their tree.
Then, with the last verse read, the final turn of a page brings back
the title page's close-up of the "darkling elf." He is now aware of
the reader (as his verse and illustration said he would be) and is
preparing to jump from fiction into the reader's own world.

   Lobel's ongoing acknowledgment of the reader's place in books, of the power of books in the reader's life, and of their overlapping benefits is an extension of his life: "Children's books always have a calming effect on me, the power to ease my spirit in troubled times. Something akin to the comfort of crackers and warm milk."[25] As he interpreted or performed the texts of others, Lobel reflected his feelings that reading and stories, if given the chance, could bring a pastoral renewal to one's daily world.

3

Returning to the Third Grade

. . . over the heads of my children.[1]

As his own children neared school age and the pressures of supporting a family grew, Lobel began to write stories for the first time since grade school. Whether his early texts grew out of stories he told his children[2] or other sources, they contained themes, character types, and images that would continue to occur and evolve throughout his work for the next twenty-six years. Mister Muster, his first character, for example, turned order topsy-turvy as would so much of Lobel's nonsense to come including *The Man Who Took the Indoors Out, Owl at Home,* and *The Turnaround Wind.*

In retrospect, Lobel believed that *A Zoo for Mister Muster* and other early books were influenced by watching cartoons with his children. Although Lobel was an award-winning painter,[3] in his initial picture books he concentrated more on the outline of characters as did cartoons than on shading, and backgrounds were left at a minimum. Yet Lobel's simplicity of illustration and design is far more an extension of Mister Muster's emotional world than merely an easy way to illustrate. The fact that his early texts often have an emotional world *to* visualize places them above cartoons, which rely on action rather than emotion for audience interaction.

Entering the World of Animals

Pictured on his title page in a cozy and stylish chair with plants nearby, Mister Muster is a direct predecessor of Lobel's home-loving characters. And like those later characters, Mister Muster's primary concern is friendship. "I only live at the end of the street," he tells his animal friends at the zoo, "But it seems far, far away when I must leave my friends."[4]

George Woods in the *New York Times Book Review* found *A Zoo for Mister Muster* to be "one of the most satisfying books" of the spring of 1962 and concluded his review by praising Lobel's "serenely humorous drawings."[5] Both descriptions can be ascribed to the body of his work as well. The sense of serenity is in large part due to Lobel's symbiotic themes of home and companionship. Such a sense of serenity is also suited to the child's dream world, a world where one can enjoy childhood pleasures with the freedom of an adult, but without the burdens of adulthood. Mister Muster, like Frog and Toad, has the sensibilities of a child, yet lives alone as an adult. This paradoxical character type is the essence of the pastoral world and dominates Lobel's work. Even his few clearly adult characters like Ming Lo and Uncle Elephant possess the emotional belief and innocent joy of a child.

Two years later Mister Muster returned as full-time zookeeper in *A Holiday for Mister Muster,* which was selected by the *New York Times Book Review* as one of the Best Illustrated Children's Books of the year. Once again friendship and home are Mister Muster and Lobel's primary concerns.

Early Tales

Lobel's next two manuscripts left the contemporary world behind (or attempted to) in exchange for castles, woods, and magic. Neither *Prince Bertram the Bad* (1963) nor *Giant John* (1964) are outstanding, but they are enjoyable and still in print. Most important, they were Lobel's first attempts to write in a folk style that, with ten more years of germination, would produce such vibrant texts as *How the Rooster Saved the Day* and *Whiskers & Rhymes*.

Prince Bertram and the narrator in *Uncle Elephant* (written seventeen years later) are Lobel's only child protagonists with book-length stories. The differences between the two books reflect the differences between issue-fiction and quality fiction, and Lobel's maturation as a writer. While Elephant child is a character of varied emotions and behaviors through whose eyes the story lives, Prince Bertram's badness is the core of the book. His primary characteristic provides the entire plot. He is bad and by the end becomes good, and that pretty much is that. It is a sound story because readers can enjoy Bertram's wickedness, but once he begins to learn his lesson the reader's interest quickly fades.

Giant John suffered similar ills in structure. Like those of *Prince Bertram the Bad,* its characters and settings were from folktales, but with none of their language or rhythms. Lobel was not yet able to give folk elements and forms fresh twists as he does in *The Rose in My Garden* (1984) or to disappear into the archetypal teller's voice as he does in *Ming Lo Moves the Mountain* (1981). Particularly when compared with his later work, *Prince Bertram the Bad* and *Giant John* suffer from what was still a rather generic voice. Both were set near the land of Bartholomew Cubbins—a character in one of Lobel's favorite childhood books—but neither were sure enough in plot or bold enough in style to claim any space of their own.

Of the two, *Prince Bertram the Bad* received the better reviews, several enjoying its tone of mock-folktale or farce. The *New York Times Book Review* pronounced it a "delightfully farcical fairy tale with good, gay illustrations."[6] *Commonweal* found the text crisp and the illustrations witty,[7] while the *Christian Science Monitor* found it to be a "hilariously funny little tale."[8]

Giant John is sweet, but having no significant conflict or at least little dramatic buildup, even its happy ending feels limp. It is not broad enough in its humor to resemble farce, nor does it connect deeply enough with any folk motifs or rhythms to sound "authentic." And, without the rich characterization of Lobel's later "I Can Read" books, *Giant John* is too thin to succeed as a vignette. Most critics ignored it or attacked it. The British publication *Junior Bookshelf* gave it backhanded praise, stating: "Really bad books, like *Giant John,* have a charm all of their own. There is a blundering naivety [*sic*] about these drawings, as about the hero himself, which is, near enough, irresistibile."[9] Master illustrator Fritz Eichenberg wrote a much warmer review in *Book Week,* finding it "endowed with a childlike and appealing humor than grows on you."[10]

Within Lobel's oeuvre *Prince Bertram the Bad* and *Giant John* are two of his least grounded works. They are two of his largest books of the period, and after working on so many "I Can Read" volumes, he seems to have been set adrift on such large pages. Both Prince Bertram and Giant John wander about in space, often without even the horizon line of an empty stage. Both stories are about family and home, but neither evokes much warmth or coziness.

Growing Fables

The same year as *Giant John,* 1964, Lobel published his first "I Can Read" text, *Lucille.* Written in the present tense, *Lucille* is a fablelike tale of identity in which a horse is transformed by place and clothing into a horse-lady. Lobel's text is again adequate, but it is best viewed as an early rehearsal for evolving themes and voice. Once the initial pleasure of changed routine wears away (the outdoors brought indoors), the pressures of ladylike behavior build until, at a disastrous tea party, Lucille chucks her false life and returns to the dusty field. She has learned, as Lobel concluded his 1980 fable "The Hen and the Apple Tree," that "It is always difficult to pose as something that one is not."[11] Home again outdoors, Lucille consumes her ladylike hat for supper.

In what would become an inherent aspect of Lobel's work, *Lucille* begins at home, ventures out, and ends at home with Lucille happy to be home because of her experience of the journey. By the conclusion all the characters—farmer, farmer's wife, pig, and Lucille—value their different kinds of homes, having gained insight from Lucille's experience.

One aspect of *Lucille* that did not become a regular element of Lobel's writing is what some might call its sexism. Lucille wants to be a lady like the farmer's wife because all she does is drink tea and listen to the radio. *Lucille* contains Lobel's usual contrast of work and pastoral leisure, but here his traditional farm setting makes it a conflict between gender roles as much as between attitudes.

The illustrations are also best viewed as rehearsals. Lobel himself later referred to the "lousy"[12] look of the colors. When compared with even the melodramatic "The Thorn Bush" in *Mouse Soup,* Lobel's thick ragged line turns his characters in *Lucille* into cartoon muggers rather than actors. Many doublespread pages contain his first gesture of framing, but it is all but pointless. The right angles of stylized flowers in the upper left- and right-hand corners decorate without purpose. There is not even the consistency of using them to represent indoor scenes as opposed to those out of doors.

Still in print, *Lucille*'s theme of being true to one's own nature is obviously stronger than its execution. But as Lobel told *Early Years* of his own reading, "the books that adults judge harshly may have great value to a child."[13]

The Bears of the Air (1965), as noted by the *Times Educational Supplement* in 1978,[14] is a moral tale for both adult and child. After Grandfather Bear chastizes his four grandsons (Ronald, Donald, Harold, and Sam) for not behaving as good, serious bears should, their playful antics save his glasses, which he needs in order to read his book, "Things a Good Bear Should Do." Once he realized that it was the cubs' "misbehaving" that saved his glasses, Grandfather Bear sees the light and joins their pastoral activities.

Reviews grumbled as loudly as Grandfather Bear. *School Library Journal* called it "a moralistic story that seems pointless and unchildlike."[15] The *Junior Bookshelf* found it a "tedious tale illustrated with revolting coyness."[16] Richard Kluger writing for *Book Week* was agressively negative: "Arnold Lobel's *The Bears of the Air* are such cuddly-wuddly butterballs that I wish the hunting season were on. . . . The bears' most prominent feature are big black rubberball noses, which I'd like to punch, they're so cute. The point of the story, as I get it, is that misbehaving bears know what's good for them better than their old-fashioned grandfather. I'm on grandfather's side."[17]

Like most of his stories to come its themes were conformity versus individuality and the regulated life versus pastoral joy or play, but the loudness of the lesson buried its truth. Like *Lucille,* the cast of characters is also a problem. Where *Lucille* became a debate over sex roles, *The Bears of the Air* becomes a contest between generations. Once again extremes between characters confuses Lobel's theme, and the debate overshadows the joie de vivre.

For Lobel this period was a far from successful, yet significant stage in his writing, proving the life in his moral written fifteen years later for his fable "The Young Rooster": "A first failure may prepare the way for later success" (*F,* 37). Traces of *The Bears of the Air*'s pastoral celebration of play and song (story, too) as "useful things to do" can be found throughout Lobel's work. And, while this book's plot is not echoed in *Fables,* four of Lobel's morals could be applied to *The Bears of the Air* as final punctuation: "Without a doubt, there is such a thing as too much order" (*F,* 2); "At times, a change of routine can be most healthful" (*F,* 5); "It is always difficult to pose as something that one is not" (*F,* 11); and "Satisfaction will come to those who please themselves" (*F,* 22).

From a variety of perspectives *Martha, the Movie Mouse* (1966) is the most significant of his early texts. It was not only his first text in verse, but also the first to explore the act of storytelling and the creative process that came to be his own: transforming one's own life into story and song. It was also a return to the theme of companionship and to human-animal fantasy, which were the heart of *Mister Muster.* And, as with *Mister Muster* and other books to come, the inside goes out and the outside comes in. Everyone, including Martha, comes inside to escape through movies. Then later Martha brings what is inside her outside—her songs and stories—to share with those who've come in from the cold.

A self-proclaimed "unrepentant anthropomorphist,"[18] Lobel's depiction of Martha is his liveliest up to that time. In many ways she seems more human than her human friend, Dan, the projectionist. Martha is so full of emotion and movement that her dance steps were reprinted in the *New York Times Book Review* along with George Woods's positive review.[19]

Others were not as enamored with Martha's story. Elva Harmon's flip review in *School Library Journal,* declaring it "a slight, purposeless story with an inexplicable ending told in stilted verse,"[20] completely misses its theme. While most would agree that it is not Lobel's best verse, Harmon failed to grasp the book's inner story of friendship and life turned into story. Writing in the *Saturday Review,* Alice Dalgliesh also failed to read beyond the surface.[21] In likening the book to Don Freeman's *Pet of the Met* (1953) she was confusing setting with theme. *Martha, the Movie Mouse* does, like Freeman's *Pet of the Met* and *Cyrano the Crow* (1960), deal with fantasy animals in the human world of show business, but that is where the similarity ends. Freeman's opera-loving mouse is such an intense fan of opera music that he leaps on stage and begins to dance. But he dances only for himself and, going unnoticed by the audience, his art is never shared. It is only with the cat's attack, before he, too, is soothed by the music, that the audience notices the animal world. The pet of the Met and his family exist in an anthropomorphic world unseen by the humans around them. *Cyrano the Crow* deals with television and a crow whose talent is impersonating the voices of others. When he finally gets his big chance at television stardom, Cyrano panics when he can't recall his own voice, flees show business, and decides to be happy just being himself.

Martha is an ardent fan of the movies just as Freeman's mouse is a fan of the opera, but that is only the first half of her story. Rather than being "invisible" to the audience or losing herself like Cyrano the crow, Martha becomes the art and artist the audience loves and in doing so finds her true home. After experiencing the forms and patterns of movie narratives, Martha is able to transform her life into songs and stories that *become* theater.

She sat down on the stage
And then,
Quite softly,
With a voice appealing
Began to sing
With heart and feeling.
She sang
A very long lament
Of garbage dumps
And cold cement.
She sang
About her sad life past,
Of alley cats
She ran from fast.
She sang of mousetraps
Tightly set
And city streets
All dark and wet.
She sang the blues,
A haunting tune
So beautiful
That very soon
The people
Were all moved to tears.
They clapped their hands
And shouted cheers.
That theater
Rocked with celebration
As Martha
Bowed to their ovation.[22]

Like Martha, Lobel began to find his widest critical and popular acceptance when he began to tell and sing of his own life. As
he later said, "I realized there was no reason why I couldn't . . .
start writing more out of my own feelings. I think that's how Frog
and Toad came to be. It [*Frog and Toad*] was the first time I

turned inward. . . . I was aware that all of the things that happened in it were essentially very personal to me and had resonances in my own life."[23] Martha and Lobel both enjoyed the pleasure of a story well told. But it was only after they experienced the essence of that pleasure—the honest sharing of human experiences—that they found their best stories and loving audiences.

Visually, *Martha, the Movie Mouse* was also a firm step in the growth of Lobel's talent. Page designs are more greatly varied than in earlier books. With more narrative action than in his previous texts, he used, by turn, isolated characters, vignettes, and framed images. As a result, page designs actively contribute to the progression and evocation of the narrative. Especially rewarding is Lobel's use of the physical page itself like a wall separating two adjacent rooms. The reader first sees the projection room with its projector beaming the film through a drawn hole in the wall. Then, with a turn of the page, the reader sees the very beam of light coming out the other side of the page (the wall) and shining over the heads of the movie audience, which fills the two-page spread. Equally effective is the two-page spread depicting Martha on stage. The corresponding text (quoted above) is printed in a narrow column on the far left, while the audience, eager to hear more, crowds toward the opposite side where Martha sits on the edge of the stage. Even the endpapers contribute to Martha's world of movies. Jet black, they signify the darkness of the movie theater. A step beyond that is the square cut out of the front endpaper. When the book is first opened, the reader sees not only the blackness of the dark theater, but also Martha's image (from the title page) like a movie itself shining on a screen.

Lobel's use of yellow, tan, and orange (preseparated colors) echos the world of movie lights and their visual warmth in the darkness. He also gives his scenes the detail and depth of film's "reality" rather than the representational stage sets of earlier books. Now setting as well as character shares the mood of the story.

The wizard in *The Great Blueness and Other Predicaments* (1968) who brings color to the world is Lobel's first protagonist who is not a child or child-substitute. The entire village, however, acts with the intensity of a child who, once discovering green, insists on everything he owns being green. On its surface *The Great Blueness* is a literary folktale with the wizard-artist creating first the primary colors and then mixing them to color the world. Within the story's action Lobel's theme cuts deeper and explores the problems of compulsiveness and absoluteness that would later plague Toad, Owl, and everyone that Grasshopper meets on the road.

After painting everything in their gray world a bright, cheerful blue, the villagers discover that blue can also be depressing. Entirely blue, the world becomes as monotonous as when everything was gray. Yellow is happy *and* painfully bright. Red is glorious *and* fosters bad tempers. Like Lobel's hippopotamus at dinner in *Fables,* the villagers learn that "too much of anything often leaves one with a feeling of regret" (*F,* 38). It is only after the wizard in *The Great Blueness* discovers that all colors can be used at once that a balanced world evolves. The villagers come to understand the value of variety and differences and the richness of the wizard's maxim: "You must take them all."[24]

As an example of folklike literature, *The Great Blueness* is much more sucessful than either *Prince Bertram the Bad* or *Giant John. The Great Blueness* has a narrative rhythm that follows the folktale pattern of recurring actions and lines, building interest and participation in the reader/listener. As he would later do with such texts as *Hildilid's Night,* Lobel effectively uses the dimensions and placement of framed images to reinforce the story's rhythms. When the villagers are happy the Brueghel-like scenes stretch horizontally across the two-page spread—open and wide. When unhappy, the villagers are shown in vertical illustrations on the right-hand page that bleed off the page. They seem as confined and troubled by their tight space as they are by the effect of the color. In contrast, the scenes of the wizard in his cellar mixing paints are small framed images that increase in size as one reads across the two-page spread and the wizard discovers something new.

The reviews were again extremely varied. *School Library Jour-*

nal found the drawings "as monotonous as the text, so color this drab."[25] Selma Lanes, however, writing in the *New York Times Book Review,* praised Lobel's attention to story and concluded by saying *The Great Blueness* "hasn't a single drab moment."[26]

As he later did with *Mouse Tales* and *The Book of Pigericks* Lobel seems to have felt a connection with the artist in *The Great Blueness.* While the published version features a full-bodied wizard of middle years and a full beard, the dummy he presented to Harper & Row[27] depicts a younger, rather impish looking wizard with only a mustache much like Lobel's own appearance at the time he created the book.

In many ways it is startling to realize that only one year passed between *Small Pig* (1969) and *Frog and Toad Are Friends* (1970). Narrative form, tense, visual style, and emotional depth separate the two. On the other hand, they are connected by a quiet, sly sense of humor, a pastoral celebration of country life, and an assertion of one's right to be one's self.

As with *Lucille, Small Pig* is written in the present tense, but it is a richer text thanks to twists—some visual, some verbal—that keep it moving to a logical, yet wholly satisfying conclusion. Small Pig's story, like Lucille's and other characters' to come, is an odyssey in miniature. He flees an overcleaned home—his mud puddle is literally cleaned away by the vacuum cleaner—suffers the wrath of swamp creatures and the horrors of a junkyard, endures the pain and embarrassment of getting stuck in cement, and finally returns home to a renewed mud puddle and happiness. The catalyst for Small Pig's adventure is the farmer's wife, the first of three fanatic housekeepers to appear in Lobel's work as comic extensions of his own passion for neatness. Small Pig would surely have run from the housefly in *Grasshopper on the Road* and would quickly nod in agreement with the moral of *Fables*'s "The Crocodile in the Bedroom" that "without a doubt, there is such a thing as too much order" (*F*, 2). Luckily for Small Pig, the farmer's wife comes to agree and begins to honor his natural manner of living.

Though Lobel uses basically the same farmer, farmer's wife, and pig from *Lucille* (Small Pig has a cameo role), his illustrations for *Small Pig* are softer in line and color. Cross-hatching adds shading and depth, and more detailed settings and a greater use of vignettes create a stronger sense of place than in *Lucille*. Characterizations are also an improvement over *Lucille*, with both humans and animals acting more often than mugging. As is appropriate for the lead character, Small Pig steals the show.

Small Pig also represents a small change in narrative form. While still a single story like *Lucille,* it is episodic, with each scene—home, swamp, junkyard, cement—dramatic in its own right, yet each building on the last. It is a growing step toward the chapter format of the *Frog and Toad* books and his best text— relaxed, solid and comfortable, yet fresh—since his two *Mister Muster* volumes.

After several years of—at best—mixed reviews, those for *Small Pig* praised both its text and illustrations. George Woods of the *New York Times Book Review* wrote: "Mr. Lobel, as always, is adept at plotting amusing predicaments and putting woebegone expressions on illustrated animal faces."[28] England's Margery Fisher found it to be both a "witty and pithy narrative."[29] Genre, voice, and creative approach all clicked in *Small Pig*. For Lobel it was a strong sure step toward his masterful books to come based on the foibles of his life and written with humor and compassion.

After *Small Pig* Lobel would no longer write of anthropomorphic animals and people in the same story. Nor with two exceptions would he ever deal with the city again. The two occasions on which he does portray the city center again on cleanliness (*On the Day Peter Stuyvesant Sailed into Town* and "The Bath" in *Mouse Tales*). Agreeing with Small Pig that rural or pastoral life is that to which he is best suited, Lobel soon took up literary residence in the garden of Frog and Toad, Owl, Grasshopper, and glorious Uncle Elephant.

4

There Was an Old Pig
Who Loved Lear

My favorite has always been Edward Lear, an interesting, amazing artist whose life and work have always haunted me.[1]

When Lobel was asked in 1977 by *Wilson Library Bulletin* to
write about his favorite illustrators, he spent eighty percent of
his space discussing the texts, illustrations, and life of Edward
Lear. His perspective of Lear's nonsense as a gift to Victorian children is in direct alignment with his own pastoral voice. "The freewheeling feverish world that Lear presented to these boys and
girls was in direct contrast to the restricted existence they knew;
the lack of moral judgments as a dramatic departure from the
other, didactic, literature they had to read."[2] In writing about nonsense poetry of the nineteenth century W. H. Auden could be describing Lobel as well as Lear when he states it is an "attempt to
find a world where the divisions of class, sex, occupation do not
operate."[3] Nonsense verse by its very nature is pastoral, and its
reading becomes an Arcadian interlude, a temporary escape—a
laughter of release—into joyful play and wonderment. The best of
Lear's work represented to Lobel the world of children's books he
longed to create: vigorous figures, economically presented comedies based on absurdities of behavior rather than public issues,

and a "tension between the simplicity of a form and the richness of content or idea."[4]

A gentle or genial nonsense is the weft of Lobel's writing from his first text, *A Zoo for Mister Muster,* to his last, *The Turnaround Wind.* Slightly absurd and contrary to socially acceptable behavior, Mister Muster turns things inside out and then back again. First, the animals leave their cages to stay in his apartment; then he leaves his apartment to stay with them in the zoo. Lobel's first two "I Can Read" texts also turn things topsy-turvy. Both the vain horse in *Lucille* and the mud-loving pig in *Small Pig* are cousins to Lear's limerick characters whom "they" harass in an attempt to enforce social conventions. Though potentially didactic in theme, Lobel's texts remained lighthearted because, like Lear, he saw himself as primarily an entertainer.

The year 1968 brought the publication of Lobel's first two picture book interpretations of material in the public domain. Though not by Lear, *The Comic Adventures of Old Mother Hubbard* is certainly connected to Lear in both form and tone and introduces elements that became classic Lobel. As Lobel would do with most of the nonsense he illustrated (his as well as other's), he set *Mother Hubbard* in Victorian England when Lear and nonsense were at the height of their popularity. Lobel's framed illustrations are paced like comic scenes between blackouts in a burlesque stage play. Their design and emotional rhythm are synchronistic with the text—an ongoing staccato flip-flop from calm to alarm, hope to disbelief. Each of the framed images, especially those of comic alarm, have the snap and lively movement of Lear's limerick illustrations. All movements are exaggerated to a point of dance, thus increasing once again the joy and absurdity of events. Published during a period of frequent folktale picture books, Lobel's *Mother Hubbard* remains one of the freshest and best. At the time of its publication Selma Lanes in the *New York Times Book Review* found it a "superior rendition."[5] Speaking at Lobel's memorial service in January 1988, James Marshall spoke of its "wit and great invention. If you are an illustrator who is considering drawing 'Old Mother Hubbard,' I advise you not to look at Arnold's version. You won't put pen to paper."[6]

Lobel's other Lear-related book of 1968 was by Lear himself. First published as one of the nonsense stories in *Nonsense Songs, Stories, Botany and Alphabets* (1871), "The Story of Four Little Children Who Went Round the World" is an eccentric adventure. It is the only time Lobel created serial illustrations for any text by Lear that Lear himself had illustrated. Lear's own pen-and-ink drawings number twenty and have been (in different editions) variously dispersed through the text. Lobel's interpretation is larger and, designed as a forty-four-page picture book with numerous doublespread images, features twenty-eight illustrations.

Except for following Lear's choice of headgear for the main characters—Violet, Slingsby, Guy, and Lionell—Lobel created his own world with detailed pencil and wash drawings. He begins their adventure in Victorian England, the period in which children first enjoyed that very nonsense adventure. The juxtaposition of absurd events with the formality of England worked well in early British comedy films. But while such films placed everyday people doing eccentric or comic acts in everyday places, Lear's story places everyday people doing eccentric acts in absurd or nonsensical places. Lear's emphasis on nonsense settings rather than behavior is possible in prose, but its visualization encounters the same problems of filming a radio fantasy. No matter what the image on paper, it is less than the reader's imagination. And, tied to the reality of page and paper, the fantastic seems less possible.

Well designed and executed, Lobel's illustrations nonetheless fall short—or still. They are often comic in content but fail with regard to what Cammaerts calls the "nonsense style in art."[7] Lobel's illustrations are so carefully designed and executed that they cannot connect with the sense of absurdity and spontaneity in the text. A picture-book edition of "The Story of the Little Children Who Went Round the World" requires images of an elderly Quangle-Wangle, millions of sneezing angry mice, crabs wearing mittens, and a giant cauliflower that walks with the aid of two "superincumbent confidential cucumbers."[8] Lobel's drawings take themselves so seriously that they cease to be nonsense and in no way seem, as nonsense images should appear, to be "improvised on the spur of the moment."⁹

As often happens with stories in the public domain, several editions of Lear's text were published within a two-year period, none of their publishers aware of the others at the time of conception. The year before Lobel's Macmillan edition, Harlan Quist had published Stanley Mack's interpretation. The same year as Lobel, even reviewed on the same page in *School Library Journal*, Walker published a curious edition that paired it with "The History of the Seven Families of the Lake Pipple-Popple." This edition featured Lear's original drawings but printed them in varying sizes and in green, orange, and pink rather than black as designed by Lear. It was the colorized edition of Lear's drawings that received the biggest nod of approval from *School Library Journal*.

As a picture book, regardless of illustrator, *The Four Little Children Who Went Around the World* seems to have failed owing to its odd length. It is at once too old for young children and too young in design for older children able to read it on their own.

Lobel's second and final effort at illustrating a text by Lear as a picture book was *The New Vestments* in 1970.¹⁰ Lear himself never published any drawings for "The New Vestments," thus leaving Lobel free to do his visual interpretation without comparison. Based on nonsense behavior rather than nonsensical setting, this text was more conducive to visualization and, as a shorter text, more suited to the picture-book format than "The Story of the Four Little Children Who Went Round the World." In a *Publishers' Weekly* interview Anita Lobel states, "In our illustrations we both like to show someone's dignity being mocked."¹¹ The "old man in the Kingdom of Tess" who invented a purely original dress is just their type of character—kind though a bit pompous and literal-minded to a dangerous degree. He is literally mocked from all sides, and Lobel marvelously evokes the pandemonium. With his original dress including a shirt of dead mice, rabbit-skin drawers, pork-chop trousers, biscuit girdle, chocolate drop buttons, and a cabbage leaf cloak, the man from Tess becomes a walking smorgasbord for all "Beasticles, Birdlings, and Boys."[12] Lobel's airy ink-line drawings are quick and playful in tone and a fine balance for the text. Even stronger is his sense of varied and cumulative page design that adds cinematic energy and drama to what is basically a plotless litany of disasters. Though warmly reviewed, including praise by Harve and Margot Zemach in the *New York Times Book Review*,[13] and the only U.S. picture-book edition of the text to date, Lobel's *The New Vestments* quickly faded from view. As fine a book as it is, it could not compete with the freshness and depth of Lobel's other book published the same year, the now classic *Frog and Toad Are Friends*.

The *Ice-Cream Cone Coot and Other Rare Birds* (1971) was Lobel's first original text obviously inspired by Lear and also his first text that was pure nonsense rather than fantasy. In *Nonsense Songs, Stories, Botany and Alphabets* (1871) (the centenary is an interesting coincidence), *More Nonsense, Pictures, Rhymes, Botany, Etc.* (1872), and *Laughable Lyrics, A Fourth Book of Nonsense Poems, Songs, Botany, Music, Etc.* (1877) Lear had created in name and image thirty-two different nonsense flowers. Bottlephorkia Spoonifolia, as an example, resembles a wild daisy (127). Manypeeplia Upsidownia resembles bleeding hearts (128), and Barkia Howlaloudia appears to be a cousin to the rabbit-faced larkspur (157). Rather than imitate Lear's plants, Lobel created rare, nonsense birds. While it is uncertain whether or not Lobel knew of Lear's "Coloured Birds" in *Queery Leary Nonsense* (1911) and *The Lear Coloured Bird Book for Children* (1912),[14] he surely knew of Lear's nonsensical botanizing and his beginning work as an excellent painter/illustrator of birds. Moving beyond basic verbal and visual identification (all Lear did for his nonsense botany and birds), Lobel also describes each species in a brief verse.

A camera becomes: The shuttercluck will never sing, nor
                      will he ever fly,
                      But he can take your picture when
                      he clicks his big round eye.[15]

A bottle of milk
becomes:

The Milkbottle Midge is a
    bird highly prized.
He is friendly and round
    and homogenized.

(18)

Door keys take
wings and:

Over our heads the Key Cranes
    are floating
Looking for doors that
    might need unlocking.

(31)

Reviews ran the gamut from the "jingles are forced"[16] in *School Library Journal* to "inspired, zany verses and pictures"[17] in *Commonweal*. The *New Yorker* recommended it, but *Horn Book* didn't review it at all. While it is far from Lobel's best or meatiest book, most reviewers failed to perceive it as verbal/visual nonsense humor in which image is as relevant as word rather than light poetry accompanied by illustrations. As Cammaerts points out in *The Poetry of Nonsense,* nonsense rhymes are by their essence forced and obvious. "The rhyme not the thought, becomes the source of inspiration, and the singer builds his story around it."[18] In *The Ice-Cream Cone Coot* Lobel is not even trying to build a story. His verses are knowingly nonsense versions of an ornithologist's descriptions. The verse naming of objects turned into birds works to heighten the nonsense by reinforcing the absurdity of any object sprouting wings.

Lobel enjoyed writing in verse. "It's very hard, but I love doing it," he told *Lion and the Unicorn.* "It's like doing the *New York Times* cross-word puzzle. It's sort of a game I like to play."[19] *Martha, the Movie Mouse* was his first published narrative verse and only one of three that are picture-book length. In the following years, as Lobel said, "to keep the pot boiling,"[20] he also wrote and illustrated light verse for *Humpty Dumpty Magazine.* These included "Owls Old and Odd" (January 1967), "The Great Rabbit

Circus" (January 1968), and "Very Strange Birds" (February 1970). The latter was the beginning of *The Ice-Cream Cone Coot* published the following year by Parents Magazine Press, which owned *Humpty Dumpty* at that time. Also during this period (specific records have been lost by both Lobel and *Humpty Dumpty*) Lobel wrote his first pig limericks, the early seeds of *Pigericks*.

Never one to repeat himself, Lobel's next book-length verse was a comic history. *On the Day Peter Stuyvesant Sailed into Town* (1971) is not nonsense in content, but it is related to Lear by genre. Comic histories were very popular in Victorian England, and Lear wrote at least two himself. While Lear wrote of the adventures of Romulus and Remus and the life and death of Caius Marius,[21] Lobel wrote about Peter Stuyvesant's success in turning New York/New Amsterdam from a broken-down village of trash into a prosperous town rivaling those in Europe.

Lobel's illustrations for *On the Day Peter Stuyvesant Sailed into Town* are some of his very best. At the same time they are sharing historical information, they are also filled with a lightness of line and content that matches the humor of the verse. Lobel's soft hues and shadings maintain the story's gentle delivery of a text that could have easily become didactic. Every page shares the zest and plumpness of the celebratory meal that concludes the book.

While Lear's contemporaries were not uniformly impressed with his comic histories,[22] Lobel's similar blend of affection and jesting was warmly received. *On the Day Peter Stuyvesant Sailed into Town* was praised in *Kirkus Reviews,* the *Horn Book,* and the *New York Times Book Review,* and Zena Sutherland in the *Bulletin of the Center for Children's Books* cheered it as an "ingenious presentation of a bit of colonial history, told in blithe verse and illustrated with pictures that are humorous and handsome."[23]

As only two of Lear's comic histories have been discovered and neither was ever published, the connection between Lear and Lobel is most likely coincidental. Yet as coincidence, the connection is of interest, for it shows kindred writers of verse and humor exploring similar paths.

With *The Man Who Took the Indoors Out* (1974) Lobel returned to nonsense and created his best book-length verse. Blending his love of home with his love of nonsense and verse, he produced a tale of pure Victorian humor in which everyday objects come to life.[24] Described in the *Children's Book Showcase, 1975, Catalog* as "a book for a mad tea party . . . a world gone lyrically beserk,"[25] it would likely have been popular during Lear's time and is Lobel's ode to Lear himself—inside and out.

In both story and verse Lear had taken the indoors out time and again. "The Four Little Children Who Went Round the World" sleep in a giant tea kettle while out to sea, and "The Jumblies" go to sea in a kitchen sieve. "The Nutcracker and the Sugar Tongs" run away forever, while "The Broom, the Shovel, the Poker and the Tongs" and "The Table and the Chair" go after adventure, then come back home. Lobel's Bellwood Bouse, drawn as Lear himself—round body, bald head, and giant beard—takes his beloved objects outside to enjoy the air.

Like the falling tree in the forest, nonsense doesn't really exist unless noticed by someone who sees the contrast with sense. As Lear's table and chair "toddled round and round"

> . . . everybody cried,
> As they hastened to their side,
> "See! the Table and the Chair
> Have come out to take the air![26]

Similarly, as homebody Bouse leads the contents of his home on a parade around the town square, people gathered to watch.

> They giggled and chuckled,
> They laughed long and loud.
> "Three cheers for Old Bouse!"
> Someone said with a shout,
> "The man who has taken
> the Indoors out!"[27]

However, once the indoors is outdoors Lobel's tale is very different from Lear's. Bouse experiences the other side of Lear's tales. Once his memory-filled objects are gone, his house no longer feels like a home. "A man's belongings," states Yi-Fu Tuan in *Topophilia*, "are an extension of his personality; to be deprived of them is to diminish, in his own estimation, his worth as a human being."[28] Rather than felicitous space, Bouse's house becomes dark and vacuous.

Bouse's indoors runs off "to the edge of the land, / way down near the shore" (19), where, set free from reality, his possessions enjoy the Victorian essence of nonsense[29]—a playful holiday—a respite by the sea.

> The sofa and tables,
> The bed and the clocks,
> Played hide-and-go-seek
> On some barnacled rocks.
> The pans and the platters,
> Each teacup and dish,
> Went out for a swim
> Like a school of odd fish.
> All of Bellwood's possessions,
> Well out of his reach,
> Watching the waves
> Wash the bright moonlit beach.
>   (19)

After Bouse spends a melancholy year alone, his objects finally return. A holiday isn't a holiday if it has no end. Nor is nonsense nonsense if it goes on forever and gains full control. The return of his objects is, of course, as nonsensical as their departure. Though it is winter and they are broken and chipped, the reunion is a time of reverie.

> The rocker danced
> All around and about
> With the man who had taken
> The Indoors out.
>   (32)

Lear, the constant traveler, forever celebrates his objects' departure. For Lobel, a self-described homebody, such departures were only the seeds of joyful reunions that celebrate home and unity.

The incongruity of Lobel's voice and narrative events also contributes to the book's world of nonsense. Possessions can't be paraded around town. And, even if they could, people leave possessions behind, not the other way around. Still, in the face of this absurdity Lobel sings of it like a lullaby and as contentedly as Bouse appears on the cover.

Lobel's pen-and-ink illustrations with three-color wash are decidedly his own, yet capture the bounce and movement of Lear's work. Bouse's world is as round and plump as a well-stuffed chair and dances from cover to final page. By either design or coincidence, the cover depicts Bouse in one of Lear's trademark poses. With one foot down and the other up and pointed out, Bellwood Bouse is as amiable and light in step as Lear's "Old Man of the Isles, / Whose face was pervaded with smiles."[30] Sharing the outdoors with the indoors, Bouse is singing the shepherd's song.

The Man Who Took the Indoors Out received praise for both its illustrations and text. The Children's Book Council selected it for the 1975 Children's Book Showcase, and the *New York Times Book Review* named it one of the Best Illustrated Children's Books of 1974. For the first time reviews spoke of Lear when applauding Lobel. Virginia Haviland in the *Horn Book* thought it to be a "nonsense poem of great virtuosity" and found that "the sheer verbal nonsense brings to mind the great Edward Lear himself."[31] England's Brian Alderson, writing in *Children's Book Review,* found it "at once amusing and touching" thanks to Lobel's "graceful and imaginative illustrations, and because of a companionable sympathy which he calls up for both the eccentric Mr. Bouse *and* for his furniture."[32] Though well received, the book "died"[33] as Lobel later said and was soon to be found only in older libraries and rare-book shops.

Lobel's personal style of nonsense began emerging in his "I Can Read" titles that were written between *The New Vestments* and *The Man Who Took the Indoors Out.* The stories of *Frog and Toad Are Friends* and *Frog and Toad Together* involve elements of nonsense and reductio ad absurdum, but it was with *Mouse Tales*

(1972) that he brought pure nonsense to his prose. Five of its seven tales are sparked by nonsense. A wishing well cries "Ouch!" when pennies are thrown in it, two mice get tossed about in the wind, another journeys so long he gets a new pair of feet, another floods his village as he naively bathes, and an old mouse succumbs to the classic burlesque gag of losing his pants in front of others. While all are nonsensical, Lobel also gives them each a touch of home and warmth. The wishing well ends up getting its wish—a pillow—from the wishing mouse who then gets *her* wish. Both windblown mice enjoy their new locations, and the mouse with the new feet calmly shows them to his delighted mother. Most indicative of Lobel's blended perspective of nonsense and the pastoral is "The Old Mouse" in which the grumpy grown-up mouse who lost his pants and dignity is finally helped by children.

Lobel's blend of nonsense and the pastoral is again expressed in "The Thorn Bush" in *Mouse Soup* (1977). The old lady mouse is not upset because she discovers a thorn bush suddenly growing out of her armchair. She is bothered because the thorn bush is sick and droopy. Yet once the policeman tends to it with water all is well. Roses soon bloom, and the old lady mouse sends him home with a joyful bouquet, the result of savoring nonsense wherever it may be found.

The world of nonsense and the creation of it vitally lightened Lear's (and the Victorian child reader's) burdens. In writing of Lear in *Wilson Library Bulletin* Lobel explained: "I think Lear knew what an important psychological outlet the creation of nonsense was for him, how necessary it was for his own particular survival . . . he was able to take much of his own torment and frustration and somehow turn it around when he wrote for children."[34] He was not plagued with Lear's lifelong repression or ill health, but to a lesser degree he could have been writing of his own work. The years in which he learned to notice the thorn bushes and nourish them into roses were the years when his writing began to flourish. Once he turned to the daily absurdities of his own life (as in the *Frog and Toad* stories), he had something lasting to share.

Nonsense was also a frequent characteristic of the texts by others he chose to illustrate during the seventies. Illustrations for these texts as discussed in chapter 2 are as varied as the stories' moods. Whether *Hildilid's Night's* dark and emphatic images or his light pencil and watercolor drawings for *Merry Merry FIBruary,* Lobel's visual delivery is consistently that of his own writing voice—deadpan and slyly tongue-in-cheek.

After an interlude of writing anthropomorphic fiction Lobel returned to human characters in his collection of folk rhymes entitled *Gregory Griggs and Other Nursery Rhyme People* (1978). It was also a return to the world of Lear-like characters. As Marcus Crouch wrote in *School Library Journal,* the characters are "portraits of strange and largely anti-social people. Here surely is the mother's milk which nourished Edward Lear."[35] The *Junior Bookshelf* of England also noticed the kinship. "The inhabitants . . . are a queer lot and they make a strange community, not unlike that created by Edward Lear. One is reminded all the time of Lear in reading Arnold Lobel's splendid collection, featuring highly individual people flouting the conventions."[36] Though he doesn't use Lear's name, Lobel's afterword well describes Lear's limerick characters and Lobel's own appreciation for outsiders. They are, he believes, "an exuberant and courageous race of human beings. In a nonsensical way they seem to mirror all of our own struggles with the rigors of contemporary living."[37]

The unity of the rhymes collected is a strong element of *Gregory Griggs,* but if we imagine them illustrated by another artist that sense of community and quality fades. With his eye attuned to Lear's nonsensical spirit, Lobel created images as lively and vivid as the rhymes themselves. He appreciates each of the characters *because* of the humanity within their seemingly absurd behavior. No matter what their deed, Lobel has drawn people like us or people we know.

It seems natural that as both an ardent fan of Lear and a lover of nonsense verse, Lobel would eventually write his own limericks. It was admiration, however, that kept the project at bay for so long. The span of time between his first published attempts at limericks and *The Book of Pigericks* was roughly fifteen years. Once he began in earnest on his own collection, he changed to "pigericks" because he didn't want to copy Lear. In his words, "if I had made them people, someone would have thought I had the audacity to imitate Lear."[38]

Beyond the differences in species, Lobel's *Pigericks* differs from Lear's book in several ways. The infamous and ubiquitous "they" so prevalent in *A Book of Nonsense* is missing from Lobel as are the references to "old." "They" is missing in large part because most of Lobel's pig characters function alone. Only two pigericks deal with direct confrontation of pig against pig. "There was a tough pig from Pine Bluff"[39] tells of school children and bullies, and "There was an old pig in a chair" (31) is a battle between husband and wife over cigar smoke.

Lear deals with challenged behavior:

> There was an old man of Dumblane,
> Who greatly resembled a crane;
> But they said,—"Is it wrong, since your legs are so long,
> "To request you won't stay in Dumblane?"[40]

or

> There was an old person of Loo,
> Who said, "What on earth shall I do?"
> When they said, "Go away!"—she continued to stay,
> That vexatious old person of Loo.[41]

Lobel in contrast deals with behavior revealed:

> There was a plain pig, far from pretty,
> Who was given to gloom and self-pity.
> But concealing her face
> Under curtains of lace,
> She then merrily strolled through the city.
>
> (28)

or

> There was a young pig who, in bed,
> Nightly slumbered with eggs on his head.
> When the sun at its rise
> Made him open his eyes,
> He enjoyed a quick breakfast in bed.
>
> (30)

Lobel may have avoided limericks with confrontations and "they" so as not to copy Lear, but he also seems to have preferred Lear's less violent limericks. Of the six limericks he chose to describe in his *Wilson Library Bulletin* article the majority focus on an individual's physical or behavioral absurdity. Only two include "they" and neither of those involve physical violence. In one of these Lobel seems to have seen even less violence than others might. When referring to the "old person of Slough"

> Who danced at the end of a bough;
> But they said, "If you sneeze, You might damage the trees,
> You imprudent old person of Slough."[42]

Lobel describes him as "cautioned by friends"[43] rather than scolded or criticized.

Lobel's pastoral voice takes him a step still further in *Pigericks*. Only twice does he refer to physical absurdity and even then the terms "stout" and "fat" are not *that* absurd for a pig. As he does in the *Frog and Toad* stories, *Fables,* and all his "I Can Read" texts, Lobel focuses on individual behavior taken to extremes. The nonsense humor in his limericks comes from the characters and their situations rather than what others do to them or think of them. The single limerick that includes a negative reaction from "they" reflects not on the main character, but on the absurd behavior of those reacting.

> There was a strange pig in the park
> Whose behavior was odd after dark.

When the full moon appeared
He grew fangs and a beard,
Which alarmed all the folk in the park.
(41)

Though far gentler in action and image than most of Lear's limericks, Lobel's still bubble with nonsense. Pigs fly à la feathers,
sneeze nieces into pieces, butter clocks, have their trousers melt
down the drain, serenade snails, grow socks that bloom flowers,
find themselves split in half, and turn themselves into the fourth
leg of a table. Lobel, as Cammaerts suggests about Lear in *The
Nonsense of Poetry,* is more interested in depicting the characters'
joy than in making an abrupt and comic twist at the end.[44] He is
also interested in creating the Victorian sense of emotional holiday—a temporary Arcadia—through nonsense humor. *The Book
of Pigericks,* indeed all of Lobel's nonsense, reveals his understanding that it is "amiable incongruity" (rather than the discom-
fort ascribed by Joyce Thomas and others[45])that, in Nancy
Willard's words, is "the secret heart of nonsense"[46] just as it is of
the pastoral.

In a turnabout of Lear's giving many of his limerick characters
his rounded pear shape, Lobel gives himself the shape of his subjects. Both first and final illustrations feature a Lobel-looking pig,
with his beloved cat Orson nearby, just as Lear frequently drew
himself with his cat Foss. In the beginning the Lobelian pig is
working at his drawing table, creating the book about to be read:

There was an old pig with a pen
Who wrote stories and verse now and then.
To enhance these creations,
He drew illustrations
With brushes, some paints and his pen.
(9)

At the book's close he is sitting in a sun-filled room with his notebook for new projects, just as he had described himself during his

From *The Book of Pigericks* by Arnold Lobel. © 1983 by Arnold Lobel. Reprinted by permission of Harper & Row, p. 8. Original dimensions 14 cm × 14 cm.

afternoons of writing in an autobiographical sketch in *Cricket Magazine for Children* in 1977[47]

> There was an old pig with a pen
> Who had finished his work once again.
> Then he quietly sat

With his comfortable cat . . .
While he rested his brushes and pen.
                    (46)

The autobiographical element is both part of the humor of the
book and part of Lobel's sense of kinship with Lear and with his
own subjects. Drawing himself as the same species as his ab-
surdly behaving subjects, he gave visualization to his belief that
a good picture book "should rise out of the lives and passions of
its creators."[48]
There are other touches of Lear, clearly in tribute rather than
imitation. With a conscious nod to his predecessor, Lobel dressed
his pigs in the attire of Lear's Victorian England.[49] Each limerick
also has a page to itself and matches Lobel's descriptions of his
own Lear volumes: "each episode has a chamber of its own, so to
speak, no crowding."[50] Where Lear used vibrant ink line and in
some editions strong vivid colors, Lobel uses lush pastels and
shading. Carefully designed and painted in full color, Lobel's illustrations still retain the air of spontaneity required of nonsense
through the gestures of his creatures and his looseness and lay-
ering of color. In addition to the incongruity of dress and species,
this contrast of high style and absurd behavior, saturated color,
and quick action creates a gallery of elegant marzipan characters
who have each in their own way dropped their pants.
Lobel has written[51] that his learning to sing humorous old
songs from the thirties such as "Shanghai Lil," "A Little Second-
hand Store," "Animal Crackers," and "I Lost my Heart on the Sub-
way" made him eager to try his hand at writing verse again.
Dedicated in part to his voice instructor and friend, John Wallowitch, *Pigericks* is a playful musicale of daily behavior heightened
to extreme for the comic stage. Most reviews were loud with ap-
plause; Doris Orgel began her review in the *New York Times Book
Review* with a tailor-made limerick:

            The talented Arnold Lobel
            Personifies pigs very well,
            Has wit, a good ear,

And reveres Mr. Lear.
No wonder these rhymes ring the bell![52]

Some, including Orgel, expressed minor disappointment in Lobel's use of "lazy" last lines that end with the same word as the first or second line. Lear, however, the acknowledged master of the form and Lobel's inspiration, was equally "lazy." As MacCann and Richard point out in their review, this repetition is also a positive element: "first, young children like the repetition, and second, the echoing effect directs the listener back to the accompanying illustration—always an important adjunct to Lear's and Lobel's verbal games."[53]

Two years after his singing debut at the 1982 American Library Association Conference in Philadelphia and later in Manhattan at the West Bank Cabaret,[54] Lobel produced his book of original verse entitled *Whiskers & Rhymes* (1985). From serenading cat on the title page to the end, Lobel sang, as the *Christian Science Monitor* stated, for his readers as he'd never sung before.[55] In its own way *Whiskers & Rhymes* is a recital—a culminating effort—that includes his best performances of what he liked best. It is a vibrant and individual response to all he had absorbed from Lear, folklore, and the songs he sang in concert. Never denying his sources of inspiration, Lobel's verses are uniquely his and all the more yeasty for their discernible genealogy. The familiar patterns, forms, and images make the verses immediately accessible while Lobel's personal voice and characters make them fresh. As with any well-rounded recital, *Whiskers & Rhymes* contains samples of all the elements and themes Lobel loved: nonsense, foibles, friendship, and home, all shared through anthropomorphic illustrations as bright and playful as the lyrics themselves. Inspired by his cat Orson (the cat in *Pigericks*), all Lobel's rhymes are illustrated with cats, though the word *cat* never appears in the text.

Once again the setting is Victorian England complete with London Bridge, parlors, peddlers, and vaudeville shows. Lobel included no limericks, but absurd behavior still fills his world of

miniature narratives. With a nod to Lear's "The New Vestments,"
he creates a costume of reverse effect:

> There was a man
> Dressed all in cheese.
> Certain was he
> That the sight would please.
> Though his neighbors agreed,
> Those clothes looked well on him,
> They ran far away
> From that certain smell on him.[56]

"They" would surely scold or exile Lobel's cat-narrator who joins
Lear's club of characters who have outsized noses, eyes, or legs.

> Boom, boom!
> My feet are large.
> Each shoe is like a garbage barge.
> Boom, boom!
> My poor head aches.
> Wherever I step, the sidewalk breaks.
>
>   (11)

Folklore also receives an honored place. With "Sing a song of
succotash" Lobel takes Mother Goose through a comic looking
glass.

> Sing a song of succotash,
> A bucketful of noses.
> And here is one for each of you,
> To help you sniff the roses.
>
>   (10)

Not only does it begin with the familiar rhythm of two Mother
Goose rhymes—"Sing a song of sixpence" and "Ring around the
rosy"—it also rhymes internally with "a pocket full" becoming a
"bucketful" of noses.

In Lobel's pastoral hands the week-long biography of Solomon Grundy becomes a comic short story of newlyweds and cooking in "I married a wife on Sunday. She cooked a wedding stew" (24). The formula of daily plot steps remains, with illness at the center. But Lobel's bride serves a pill on Wednesday and buttered bread the next day. By Sunday all is well again, and rather than dying like Grundy, the new couple celebrate their love and good health with an anniversary kiss in bed.

With "Mirror, Mirror, over the sink" (21) Lobel offers a cat-child recreating the rhyme of Snow White's wicked stepmother in much the same way middle-grade children create their playground parodies. Half the fun is in knowing the "original."

> Mirror, mirror, over the sink,
> What do you see when I take a drink?
> One nose, one mouth, two eyes that blink.
> How you'd love this face if you could think!
>
> (21)

"Mirror, Mirror" is also an excellent example of how Lobel's illustrations are, as is usually true of nonsense, vital to the verse's full effect. The verse itself is certainly clear and enjoyable, but when combined with the image of the Victorian cat-child at the bathroom mirror the sense of parody and play becomes much stronger.

The "old woman of long ago" could have appeared in classic editions of Mother Goose for she seems to be the mother of nonsense itself.

> There was an old woman of long ago
> Who went about her mending.
> She sewed the wind against the clouds
> To stop the trees from bending.
> She stitched the sun to the highest hill
> To hold the day from ending.
>
> Her thimble and threads were close at hand
> For needlework and quilting,

For sewing gardens to the sky
To keep the blooms from wilting,
For lacing the land to the crescent moon
To save the world from tilting.

                                        (46)

Her behavior is absurd, but valuable. We may laugh at her actions, as we do those of Don Quixote, all the while admiring the sincerity of her efforts and beliefs. Regardless of the absurdity, it is somehow comforting to think of someone who is willing to spend her days keeping the world we love in order.

Far from only nonsense, *Whiskers & Rhymes* is also a collection that sings of love in many of its forms. "Orson Porson, / Pudding and pie" (17) reflects Lobel's love of his cat Orson, while its illustration creates a second level of father and prodigal son. In only twenty-five words Lobel shares the safety and love that family pictures bring to a child in bed waiting for sleep.

Little pictures
Hang above me.
Pictures of the folks
Who love me.
Mom and Dad
and Uncle Jack,
They love me . . .
I love them back.

                                        (13)

Love on occasion is unrequited, as in Lobel's feline version of the film of *The French Lieutenant's Woman,* complete with an illustration of Jeremy Irons pining over Meryl Streep as the waves splash against the jetty.[57]

She listens to the waves resound,
She gazes at the sea.
I wish that she would turn around
And simply smile at me.

                                        (26)

For another couple in "It rains and it pours" (17) love is such a joyful thing they skip the chores to go laughing and dancing in the rain.

As in Lobel's "I Can Read" texts, one object stands out—the book. The love of reading is so vital to Lobel that it is as prevalent a theme as home. The cat-child admiring his family's pictures has a book beside his bed, and "Sleeping Charlie in his chair" (37) takes flight as he dreams of the journeys within the book he was reading. *Whiskers & Rhymes*'s most startling illustration comes near the physical center of the book and is also an image of reading. One quickly turns the book on its side because the illustration of stacked books is so tall it needs both pages, end to end, to include all the treasures.

> Books to the ceiling, books to the sky.
> My piles of books are a mile high.
> How I love them!
> How I need them!
> I'll have a long beard by the time I read them.
> (30)

Whether short chants about pickle paste or narrative tales of mail received, Lobel's rhymes of whiskered creatures sing a song of holidays—a playful dance at noon. They share what Lobel always experienced when he read his favorite picture books—a rest beneath Arcadia's tree.

Ethel Heins's *Horn Book* review grasped the book's zestful connection with Lear. "Unifying the illustrations is a rare combination of beauty, innocence, an understated wistfulness, and the droll, deadpan humor reminiscent of Edward Lear."[58] They are easily Lobel's most vibrant illustrations up to this time. Matching his own description of Lear's drawings, his figures are "so vigorous that they are ready to jump off the page."[59]

Just as the content of the verses covers his primary themes and images (song, home, reading, flowers, and friendship) in a celebratory manner, Lobel's illustrations bring together the best of his techniques in a cumulative style. In *Whiskers & Rhymes* he blends the brilliant colors of *Fables* and the quick looseness of

Gregory Grigg's line to create a joyful dance for the eye. Lines never stop moving and colors continually form new chords. Still, each verse is given an illustration that matches its tone. While "Postman, postman, / Ring my bell" (44) is filled with spring air and soft pastels, "Little pictures / Hang above me" (13) is as muted and warm as the cat-child's quilt. Regardless of content and tone, each illustration belies Lobel's piles of tracing-paper drafts and appears to have been created as spontaneously as the rhymes are said.

As he had done in both *Gregory Griggs* and *Pigericks,* Lobel illustrates many verses in multiple frames as if they were films. It is particularly effective with the mini-narratives "I married a wife on Sunday" (24), "Mistress Pratt" (42), and "Clara, little curly locks" (18). The series of visual changes intensifies the broad humor as in burlesque theater or silent film acting where the drama is expressed through a series of highly gestured scenes. One verse, "If you were a pot, / And I were a pan" (41), is even presented as a two-scene playlet by cat-children in costume. Nearly all the verses and their illustrations share the comic innocence and innate humor of such child-crafted plays as existed in Lobel's own childhood of cellar and bedsheet theater. This is not to say *Whiskers & Rhymes* is childish or amateurish, but rather that the artist has maintained the freshness of the child's eye while combining it with the maturity of training and the richness of adult insight.

In the *New York Times Book Review* poet Nancy Willard asked herself what children will take from *Whiskers & Rhymes*. Her answer not only points to a primary element in Lobel's voice, but also to how that element makes his voice different from Lear's. Beyond rollicking verse, Willard believes children will take "the mystery at the heart of the commonplace, the secret lives of pots and pans, needles and threads, brooms and bread."[60] Both Lear and Lobel share what Thomas Carlyle described as imaginative sympathy—"tender fellow-feeling with all forms of existence"[61]— and bring humorous animation to the world of objects. Their differences spring from their approach to objects; this affected their stories and verses as surely as it reflected their views of home.

Lear lived apart from his objects and so gave them life. His animated objects never belong to anyone and are never missed. They have no human connection. Lobel, however, like Wright Morris in *The Home Place,* found beauty and life in the commonplace.[62] Because he found daily objects beautiful, his experience of them was aesthetic, allowing him to enter the selves of the valued objects and find the life already within them.

The Turnaround Wind, the last book Lobel wrote and illustrated, contains the essence of his brand of nonsense based on incongruous juxtapositions in our daily lives. It also contains the kernel of his pastoral view: perspective changes everything. The world of *The Turnaround Wind* is one in which, even in our differences, we are literally one. For the length of the turnaround wind there is no up or down, no right or wrong.

On a summer afternoon a wide range of characters are out "walking and talking and taking the air."[63] Suddenly a giant wind comes up and everything and everyone is turned around. At this point the reader must physically keep turning the book around to read the next part of the story. The following twenty illustrations are all of two different characters at once, each character becoming another when the book is turned upside down. During the time of the turnaround wind a lovely lady is also a comical duck, a baby is a thief, and an artist is his painting. Two separate images exist as one. Ending as quickly as it began, the wind moves on leaving everyone a bit ruffled, but back in the sun. And true to Lobel's tradition, at "sunset they all went home for supper" (31).

Those overzealous about finding connections with Lear might conclude that Lobel's tale of mixed-up characters was sparked by Lear's later tale "The Adventures of Mr. Lear, the Polly and the Pussybite." While both narratives begin with characters going for a walk and involve a mix-up, the similarities quickly end. Lear's characters are literally pulled apart and put back together out of order. The Polly gets Lear's legs, the Pussybite gets Lear's stomach, and Lear gets the Polly's body. The characters are mixed up both on the page and in the story. Still, no matter how one holds the book, Lear's pictures reveal the same image. Lobel's book is the reverse. None of his characters are physically mixed up within the story, but the illustrations of them experiencing the turnaround wind *are* mixtures.

Lobel did not remember ever seeing Lear's story,[64] and it is most likely he hadn't. It has been printed in only one little-known volume, *Teapots and Quails* (1953), and then only in England. With its design of two faces in one, one when the book is rightside up and another when it is upside down (terms made nonsense by the images themselves), *The Turnaround Wind* seems more a descendant of Gustave Verbeck's *Upside-Down* cartoons of the early 1900s and Peter Newell's *Topsy-Turvys* (1893) in which every character's face is actually another when turned upside down.

Lear and Lobel's different perspectives on journeys and home are also once again made clear by contrasting these two stories. Lear's characters (including himself) begin their outing without any reference to home or setting of any kind. And, in the end, he sends his characters (still mismatched) into a deep hole from which they "are never seen or distinguished or heard of never more afterwards."[65] While Lear is divisive, Lobel is more the synthesist. *The Turnaround Wind* opens on a warm sunny afternoon in a meadow and concludes with everyone going safely home. The time in between, although darkened by clouds, is equally pastoral; all characters are equal and literally the balancing complement of one another.

In his essay "How Pleasant to Know Mr. Lear" G. K. Chesterton praised Lear for creating nonsense worlds outside our own that still feel like home.[66] Lobel would surely have agreed. He wouldn't have promised to take his volumes of Lear with him if the house burned down unless they felt like home.[67] However, when it came to Lobel's own writing he had neither need nor interest in visiting such places as the great Gromboolian plain or the hills of the Chankly Bore. He knew a nonsense world already exists within our own home-world if we only have the eyes and heart to see it— a world at once as nonsensical *and* pastoral as the Quangle-Wangle's hat in which all can live in melody and celebrate in song.

5

Frog and Toad Can Read

I will be moving on. I will be doing new things.[1]

By 1970 the early-reader genre had existed for over twelve years and included texts by authors such as Dr. Seuss, Elsa Minarik, and Nathaniel Benchley. The fall season of that year, however, brought a new level of quality and resonance of voice to the genre with the publication of *Frog and Toad Are Friends*. Praised for its depth and clarity of text and for its excellent illustrations, *Frog and Toad Are Friends* was selected as a 1971 Caldecott Honor Book and was a final contender for the Children's National Book Award. By the time its first companion volume, *Frog and Toad Together,* was published two years later, Frog and Toad had established themselves as lively, distinct, and cherished characters in children's literature. *Frog and Toad Together* was selected as a 1973 Newbery Honor Book, the only one of its genre to receive such an award for writing. Critics reached back to *Jeremy Fisher* and *Wind in the Willows* for comparisons and began to speak of Lobel's books as modern classics.

Such lush early praise often fades with time as rereadings find weaknesses and changing tastes bring new perspectives. Frog and Toad have done more than weather any test of time. They are among the few twentieth-century characters in children's literature assured an audience in the next century. Their stories are known by the majority of grade school children in the United States and have been translated into over a dozen languages. Through changing times in both publishing and social concerns Frog and Toad have proven themselves classics as Ezra Pound defined the term in his *A B C of Reading:* ". . . not because it conforms to certain structural rules or fits certain definitions. . . . It is classic because of a certain eternal and irrepressible freshness."[2]

Among the deserved early praise was Margery Fisher's review published in England, encouraging a ban on the type of symbol-hunting academics are wont to do with classics: "Does this mean that in the future students will be writing theses on the psychiatric implications of the fable in reconciling the irresponsible and irrational impulses in all of us, or on the justification of dressing the animals in green and brown suits. . . ? I hope no such dreary academic fate is in store for these two splendid comedies. I hope readers will be content to share in the sheer enjoyment behind the stories and appreciate the author's skill."[3] Nothing would be literally as breath-taking as shrouding Lobel's pastoral world of humor and joie de vivre in psychological theory. Any building up of such theories to explain Frog and Toad, no matter how well researched or well intended, would deaden their song as surely as did the characters in the Jewish folktale who wrapped the simple reed flute in beaten gold. In their effort to honor its music, they destroyed its ability to create the very music they were honoring.

Still, the lasting and unique qualities of Frog and Toad invite discussion about how they (both as characters and volumes) relate to literary traditions and, as with all touchstone books, how they came to extend and enhance those same traditions. As a pastoral world, Lobel's literary works may be most effectively explored in a like manner—with lightness, receptivity, and a sense of sharing.

The Pastoral

With regard to form, setting, theme, character, and voice few books, especially children's books, have been as thoroughly pastoral in the manner of the genre's earliest examples as the four *Frog and Toad* volumes. Lobel's vision was inherently pastoral, the natural genre for the primary themes introduced in his early work: be one's self, let others be themselves, and celebrate the coexistence of incongruities. Still, in those initial titles the pastoral had been only part of a debate of city versus country. The protagonists of both *Lucille* and *Small Pig* try out and then reject urbanity in favor of the joys of country living and their natural selves. In *The Bears of the Air* the cubs are initially chastised but then convince their rigid, achievement-oriented grandfather that their Arcadian life-style of play and song is the best way to live.

When Lobel began transforming his memories of the Vermont summers and of his children's childhoods and pet toads into stories, he found much more than just a "literary mouthpiece."[4] He discovered the pastoral setting that completed his vision, allowing him to move lock, stock, and barrel into Arcadia. Once there, the pastoral or country was no longer an element of debate, but a place of gentleness in which to explore other themes. Lobel, his writing, and his characters all began to grow strong in the warming sun.

Form

While the silver-tongued words and elaborate forms of several generations pulled the pastoral farther and farther from its roots of simple shepherd's song, Lobel's use of the "I Can Read" gave the pastoral genre a renewing journey home. Whether one prefers the term idyll, little pictures, sliver, or vignette, his *Frog and Toad* stories are the essence of the pastoral's inner duality and brevity of outer form. Brief in both length and length of clock-time covered, the stories' dominant use of dialogue quickly establishes the characters' contrasting personalities, echoing the friendly rivalry of Theocritus' shepherds. The natural use of pictures in the "I Can Read" books affected form as well. Allowing the inclusion of pastoral images, it simultaneously allowed the exclusion of long prose descriptions. Intimate in tone and often small in dimension, Lobel's illustrations—usually vignettes themselves—quickly evoke the pastoral world and let his prose focus on character and emotion. This blending of "I Can Read" and pastoral creates an aggregate that far exceeds the sum of its parts. It is startling to realize that the rich and varied world of Frog and Toad is represented by only four slender volumes. For Lobel, as well as for readers, Frog and Toad quickly took on a life beyond the printed page.

Setting

One first knows he has reached the pastoral world of Arcadia in the *Frog and Toad* series through his senses, just as Mole and Ratty in *The Wind in the Willows* know their homes and riverbanks. It is an inviting place of flora and fauna, filled with a sense of gentle light and coziness. Each volume begins with a cover framed by muted flowers and plants in gentle greens and browns made all the more tactile through pencil shadings and a lightly sketched ink line. It is classic pleasance, a natural and sensual setting midway between the rigid gray city and the violent, sexual wildwood of Rousseau's bright canvases. Lobel's muted tones establish an underlying sense of stillness and safety—the stasis indicative of the pastoral—that exists no matter what the stories' events.

Lobel's two previous early readers (*Lucille* and *Small Pig*), like the "I Can Read" texts he had illustrated for others, were single stories, darker in line and most often opaque in color. He later said that it simply took time and experience to learn that the genre was most pleasing when the illustrations were muted.[5] But with *Small Pig,* published just a year before *Frog and Toad Are Friends,* it was surely his aesthetic instinct and new cohesive pastoral vision that told him the *Frog and Toad* stories required a softer world. His illustrative eye was growing in tandem with his writing voice.

The symbiotic contribution of Lobel's illustrations to the total sense of pastoral in the *Frog and Toad* books is easily seen by looking at *The Frog and Toad Pop-up Book* (1986). The cover illustration is a repeat of the cover from *Frog and Toad Are Friends,* and most other illustrations are echoes of the original volumes. The pop-up volume, however, is in full color, presenting on shiny paper vibrant images filled with spring and action. Though Toad remains subdued, worldly Frog has traded his tweed jacket for a bright red one and his pants are now electric stripes. Emotionally, the pop-up illustrations are *in* the sunshine rather than under the shade of the Arcadian tree. Had all four volumes originally been done in such full color, a large portion of their pastoral mood, especially its quiet gentleness, would have been lost. The differences between editions again point to Lobel's instinct for finding the right tone or mood for a book. The very nature of the pop-up book cries out for brighter color to match the physical nature of the activity. It would have floundered if illustrated in the more subdued manner of the original volumes.[6]

The content of each cover and title page illustration of the *Frog and Toad* series affirms their world of classic pastoral otium, beautifully encapsulated in Toad's list in *Frog and Toad Together*:

> Wake up
> Eat Breakfast
> Get Dressed
> Go to Frog's House
> Take walk with Frog
> Eat lunch
> Take nap
> Play games with Frog
> Eat Supper
> Go to Sleep.[7]

The cover of *Frog and Toad Are Friends* (the first image readers see) is amazingly similar in design to Perugino's pastoral painting

Apollo and Marsyas, circa 1496.[8] While Perugino depicts Marsyas playing the flute for Apollo, Lobel shows Toad reading aloud to Frog. Reading is the one thing Toad is forever doing that is not on his list, and its exclusion is appropriate. As David Young states in *The Heart's Forest,* Arcadia is a poet's land, a "realm of the imagination where the composing of verses and songs was a natural activity, and where poetic values were taken for granted."[9] Within Lobel's pastoral world reading is as basic as the shepherd playing the flute. It is a world that instinctively honors writing and reading as the activities of play they truly are. To Lobel, Frog and Toad's world is largely pastoral because they *do* read and make stories and because reading itself (like the *Frog and Toad* books themselves) is an entrance into the pastoral.

On succeeding covers Frog and Toad share a bicycle built for two (the most modern object in any of the volumes), build a snowfrog, and fly a kite. Their title and contents pages continue to define their world (as do images behind opening film credits) as clearly one of pastoral otium and art or creative idleness. Frog continues to read aloud. They drink endless cups of tea and share a toddy by the fire. They go for walks, and, as Kenneth Grahame would say, "mess about in boats" with Toad reading and Frog fishing. Toad paints Frog's portrait and then *both* read books. Reading and painting both take place in the shade of a tree, the classic location of the flute-playing shepherd.

By the first words of each volume, the child reader, though completely unaware of any pastoral tradition or symbolism, knows that the world of Frog and Toad is one of joyful play, friendship, and creativity. And, with Frog and Toad the only characters depicted till the third volume, their world is also the child's vision of Arcadia—a world of childhood pleasures and priorities (eating, playing, story, and friends), but without any meddling adults. As child substitutes Frog and Toad share a world free of both child and adult roles. It is this element that marks these works' initial distinction from the fine texts of Minarik, Hurd, and others. These writers replicated the child's daily world of children and parents. Lobel, however, gives life to the child's fantasy world of equality and freedom. Again, as with most of his work, he dis-

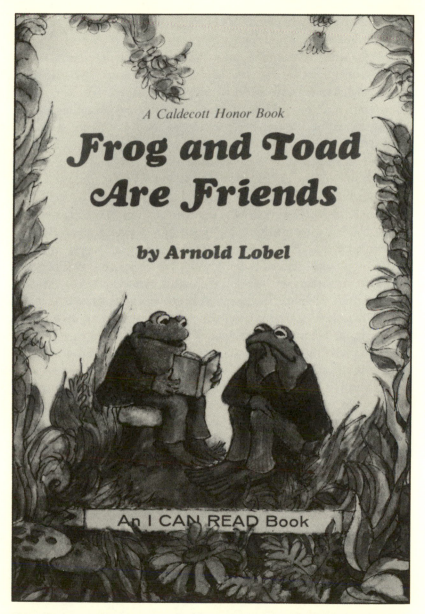

A Caldecott Honor Book

Frog and Toad Are Friends

by Arnold Lobel

An I CAN READ Book

From *Frog and Toad are Friends* by Arnold Lobel. © 1970 by Arnold Lobel. Reprinted by permission of Harper & Row, cover. Original dimensions 21.6 cm × 14.8 cm.

mantled the wall between children and adults by focusing on their shared inner concerns.

Lobel's sense of Arcadia goes, as did Kenneth Grahame's, beyond geographical landscape to include home as well. As Lois Kuznets discusses in regard to *The Wind in the Willows,* home also exists for Frog and Toad (and Lobel) as *the* felicitous space. Home is not for hiding, but for serving as one's *locus amoenus* from which "one may safely venture out into the vast universe of thought and feeling."[10] And venture they do. As Toad's list shows, one of their daily and valued activities is walking—not merely to get from here to there, though they do a good deal of that, but walking as a philosophy of life. Except for their encounter with a snake in "Dragons and Giants," Frog and Toad do not have significant physical adventures. But as Kenneth Grahame wrote in his essay, "The Romance of the Road," the walk can take the mind over greater distances than can a car through a dozen countries.[11]

This sense of home, journey, and growth is reflected in each volume's cycle of stories as well as in the individual stories themselves. Each volume begins with a story of either Frog or Toad going to visit the other. Middle stories feature shared activities. By the final or next-to-final story they have separated, but only to be reunited with an intensified sense of friendship by the end of the book. Their friendship is as much their home as their houses are and as such also a form of felicitous space.

Their frequent journeys away from home bring frequent returns. To enter or re-enter the cottages of Frog and Toad is to experience the essence of the books' literary form, the idyll, which Martha Shackford says is "known by the mood that it awakens . . . they throw one into a mild state of peace and content, rousing only those sentiments which are tranquil . . . where no tragic elements enter."[12] Lobel creates their idyllic homes by blending the intimacy of everyone's memory of a childhood home with the visual elements of the pastoral tradition. Their cottages, like the shade of a tree, are just large enough for one's self and a visiting friend. Furniture is limited, but nicely stuffed, and food, especially tea, is always just a reach away. Flowers both cut and potted are kept throughout both homes, and wallpaper is either thickly striped as if grass or floral as if a garden. The blend of noonday sun and tree shade becomes the warmth of the fireplace tucked in shadows. The one other object found through the four volumes is the book—Lobel's Arcadia (reading) within Arcadia (home) within Arcadia (the pastoral or garden setting).

If not walking or sitting by the fireplace savoring its physical and emotional warmth, Frog and Toad are most likely to be found sitting near a window enjoying the pastoral view. Here Lobel's framed illustrations and vignettes function as windows themselves. They offer the reader a selected view of the pastoral world just as the windows in the illustrations do for Frog and Toad.

Theme: Friendship

While Frog and Toad's homes are pastoral and idyllic in atmosphere, it is what they do within their dwellings that makes them truly Arcadian or felicitous space. Home is where they serve one another endless cups of tea, share stories, feel scared *and* brave together, give each other gifts, and perhaps most important of all, are simply and vitally there for one another. They create their Arcadian home *between* and *out of* themselves. As William Blake writes in *The Marriage of Heaven and Hell:* "The bird a nest, the spider a web, man friendship."[13]

Friendship is an inherent element of the pastoral idyll, and it is Lobel's masterful sharing of such friendship in conjunction with his setting that distinguishes the *Frog and Toad* volumes from most other picture books that speak of friendship. As a *New York Times Book Review* critic wrote in 1976; "Frog and Toad's friendship is not a thing; it is a mood."[14] It is a mood so complete that Lobel never needs to discuss it. While most picture books about friendship (including many fine ones) deal with the issues of making friends, fighting and making up with friends, or losing friends, Lobel evokes Frog and Toad's friendship by dramatizing their daily lives. In this he is again true to his literary genre, for the pastoral focuses not on the search, separation, and winning of love, as does romance, but on friends and lovers united in cel-

ebration. Frog and Toad frequently hold different opinions, and
Toad is at times insecure regarding their relationship, but their
friendship is solid. Archetypal homes, like their friendship, are
tested only by outside elements, and there are none (no wild
woods of stoats and weasels) near Lobel's Arcadia.

Theme: Gifts

Lobel instinctively adds great depth and completeness to Frog
and Toad's pastoral world by having them constantly give gifts to
one another. As with Virgil's shepherds, their exchange of gifts is
"a poise, a suspension, between difference and likeness, between
sharing and self-assertion."[15] Toad's gifts to Frog range from the
tangible—cookies and button-covered jacket—to the emotional
and aesthetic as when he reads to Frog and paints his portrait.
Though Frog does give Toad a hat, seeds, and a clock (indicative
of his role as organizer), his most beautiful and personal gifts are
words. It is Frog who writes Toad the letter he has longed for and
who is able to create stories that, in turn, help Toad rest, feel the
freshness of spring, and at night, the delicious and safe shivers of
a horror tale. Frog and Toad also each give to the other as they
listen to the other's stories. "The one who offers to hear our dream
or our story," states John Rouse in *The Completed Gesture,* "opens
a source of creative energy that brings us to the threshold of a
secret power and magic, that puts us in touch with our own
mystery."[16]

The epitome of their gift giving is related through "The Surprise" in *Frog and Toad All Year.* To a degree reminiscent of O.
Henry's "The Gift of the Magi," Lobel's story focuses on the joy of
giving as an act of love, rather than on romanticized or acknowledged sacrifice as proof of love. Both Frog and Toad want their
gift of raking the other's leaves to be a surprise. Thanks to the
wind, both return home to yards still needing to be raked and
neither receives the gift from the other. Yet both have given themselves a gift by the gesture of giving. "That night / Frog and Toad
/ were both happy / when they each / turned out the light / and
went to bed."[17]

All that remains is the gesture—the act itself—which is as vital to a friendship as the actual gift given. "The very form of the exchange," states Ronald Sharp in *Friendship and Literature,* "creates a spirit that can be seen as both the environment in which the exchange occurs and, ultimately, the most important thing that is exchanged."[18] Aware of the value and pleasure of giving experienced by the giver and that the gesture itself is the truest gift, both Frog and Toad are graceful gift-receivers, a role as vital to the ritual as the giving.

What Frog and Toad ultimately give themselves through their exchange of gifts is an Arcadian landscape of the mind that is reflected in the actual gifts they share. Befitting the seclusion of their pastoral setting, gifts are usually of their own making. Their Arcadia, like Lobel's, is not found, but created.

Character

Lobel's characterizations of Frog and Toad contribute to the completeness of their pastoral idyllic world as thoroughly and as intuitively as do his illustrations. "Explicitly or implicitly," states Lore Metzger in *One Foot in Eden,* the pastoral embodies antitheses "between art and nature, country and city, otium and negotium, retirement and active life, leisure and work, summer and winter, happiness and melancholy, energy and acedia, past and present, communality and alienation."[19] Frog and Toad are literally the pastoral personified. Toad is a slug-a-bed, while Frog is forever saying "Let's go!" Bucolic Toad hates housework, while Georgic Frog, the gardener, sees the same task as home*making.* Toad is impulse, while Frog is reason. Toad is of the moment, while Frog is of the past—thus his ability to tell stories. Toad is often melancholy, while Frog is usually jubilant. Toad is forever insecure about everything (from seeds to companionship), while Frog is sure (perhaps too sure) of himself and his world. Toad is perpetually innocent, to both his benefit and loss, just as Frog is equally worldly.

Still neither character is merely a cardboard symbol. Toad is not *just* a schlemiel, nor Frog *always* the wise sophisticate.

Though he cannot create a story and is forever bumbling, Toad is the reader, painter, baker, and tailor of the two. Frog has the organization and industry to grow a garden, create a story, and write a letter, but at times (as with cookies) he reaches boring levels of order and self-discipline. Lobel even came to refer to Frog's "cruel streak because he is in such command of himself."[20] Actually cruel or not, Frog and Toad each need the other for balance and completeness. Each gives value and definition to the other. They live as Thoreau said of friends in *A Week on the Concord and Merrimack Rivers,* not merely in harmony, but in melody, not in perpetual agreement, but in a pleasing sequence of interrelated contrasts.

In their ongoing relationship of opposites, both between themselves and between joint activities (i.e., reading versus walking), Lobel not only creates the pastoral balance of contradictions, but also what Sharp calls the essence of friendship: "the paradoxical combination of relaxation and excitement."[21] Within the world of Frog and Toad, Arcadia and friendship are synonymous.

It is the balance of differences and tensions that gives the *Frog and Toad* volumes their depth and allows them to be cozy and warming without being coy or saccharine. Their final story, "Alone," refracts against the entire series. Once again feeling insecure about their relationship, Toad panics when Frog wants to be alone for a while. Feeling that a monolithic friendship of constant agreement and togetherness is the only kind, Toad allows his Arcadian world—his peaceful inner landscape—to be temporarily destroyed *by* his panic. Convinced that differences mean disaster, he eventually brings disaster by denying differences. His constricting perspective has as much, perhaps more, power to destroy his pastoral friendship as anything else. He forgets (being of the moment rather than of memory) the times *his* differences in perspective—in "The Swim," "Cookies," "Down the Hill," and "Tomorrow" (one per volume)—left Frog standing alone as Toad left the scene is disagreement.

The final line of "Alone" expresses what all preceding stories had shown, what Toad had forgotten, and what makes Frog and Toad pastoral characters: "They were two close friends / sitting alone together."[22] Their differences can and must coexist if their Arcadia is to flourish. And, when both remember that truth, they are able to share the deepest moments of friendship, those that need no words. Such are the moments of waiting for Toad's letter with their arms around each other, of being silently brave in respective hiding places, and of celebrating Christmas in silence by the fireplace. They are "alone together" on their island—their personal Arcadia—just as Lobel literally drew them in the final image of their final book.

Voice

As do his textual and visual contents, Lobel's voice contributes significantly to Frog and Toad's pastoral world. To a degree, short sentences and little or no description are required by the early-reader genre. But while most early-reader texts read with the rhythm of a telegram message, Lobel's texts are even better when read aloud. As he did with other genres or forms, he found more within the "limitations" than others found without them. The genre's use of repetitive structures, phrases, and words can easily become painfully boring and comically bad as with many basal readers. Lobel, however, turned what seemed to be less into more. Rather than surrendering to the need for repetition and writing "down," Lobel (his love of music was surely influential) instinctively used repetition to create a more lyric tone, which contributed to his pastoral voice. As Rosenmeyer states in *The Green Cabinet,* pastoral anaphora (planned repetition) "calms and soothes" and its "musical repeats and doublets help to secure the otium."[23] Never using a controlled vocabulary,[24] Lobel approached the genre as a form and style rather than as a verbal workbook or lesson: "I have total freedom, and the only harness is that I am aware as I work that I'm doing a reader,"[25] by which he meant form.

Annie Dillard's description of plain writing in *Living by Fiction* well describes Lobel's prose and how it rises in quality above most texts of the genre. All early-reader texts avoid complex sentences

and limit use of adjectives and adverbs. The key difference in Lobel's prose is his approach and eye. Part of plain writing's "politeness to readers is based on respect; this prose credits readers with
feelings and intelligence. It does not explain events in all their
ramifications; it does not color a scene emotionally so that a
reader knows what he should feel. . . . This prose is humble. It
does not call attention to itself but to the world."[26] Imagine the
Frog and Toad stories rewritten in the style or tone of Steig or
Seuss and their "simple," open charm disappears. The *Frog and
Toad* stories, like the reed flute's song, are a call to the Arcadian
meadow rather than a call for attention to themselves or their
singer.

The humor of comic play has always been a part of the pastoral,
for it celebrates life. With Frog and Toad Lobel's voice became a
rich harmony of pastoral and comedy, each contributing to the
other. The appreciation of coexisting opposites (i.e., Frog and
Toad themselves) and incongruities that is the base of the pastoral is also the heart of Lobel's comic perception. As Bernard
Schilling discusses in *The Comic Spirit:*

> To a discerning man looking out upon the world, the va-
> rieties of human absurdity must appear endless. Seeing
> the many forms of vanity and hypocrisy; self-deception;
> unconscious violation of proper, sensible behavior; and
> on all sides the laughable incongruity between saying
> and doing—observing these things a man may respond
> in a number of ways. He may be indifferent, contemp-
> tuous, amused, or indignant, refusing to absolve man-
> kind for its weak failure to be what it should be. Or he
> may think of himself as sharing like other men in the
> weakness that his intelligence perceives, and so end[s]
> in a mood of tolerance—his laughter tempered by sym-
> pathy. He then sees life from both within and with-
> out, combining thought and feeling, discernment and
> tolerance.[27]

Seeing himself as sharing the often absurd behavior he wrote
about—"All the *Frog and Toad* stories are based on specific things

From *Frog and Toad are Friends* by Arnold Lobel. © 1970 by Arnold Lobel. Reprinted by permission of Harper & Row, p. 62. Photographed from the artist's original pen and ink drawing with gray wash and pencil highlights: 7 cm × 11 cm.

in my life"[28]—Lobel was able to create through humor an Arcadian world for both himself and his readers.

Seeing himself as at one with his characters—"I wanted a dialogue to go on between two characters who were essentially me talking to myself"[29]—Lobel based his humor on recognition of behavior rather than on gags and jokes. It is impossible to share the laughter of a Frog and Toad story without telling the entire story. Frog and Toad are not like the Cat in the Hat, comic characters in and of themselves, but rather characters whose actions, like our own, often become humorous. Nor are they television "sitcom" characters whose witty lines could be said in any episode. As I discussed in chapter 1, Lobel's primary comic plot is behavior based reductio ad absurdum with its snowballing rhythm of one to infinity, of logic stretched to irrationality, of molehills turned into mountains. It is not just that Toad cannot think of a story to tell ill-feeling Frog. He worries and literally beats himself to such a frazzle that *he* must take to his bed and have Frog tell *him* a story. Naturally the story Frog tells him is all about Toad's recent absurd behavior. The very fact that it *is* such extreme behavior allows one to laugh and even feel refreshed because he knows, by their level of self-dramatizing, as Rosenmeyer states of Theocritus' *Idylls,* "that the suffering cannot be profound, and that the zest of living and the penchant for pleasure will win out."[30]

Frog and Toad and George and Martha

The series of books that comes nearest Lobel's *Frog and Toad* volumes in regard to friendship as theme and humor as style are James Marshall's six titles about George and Martha, those "two great chums" who happen to be hippos. Both series are of high quality and great popularity. Both are also written in short episodes that cut beneath the surface into more complex emotions. With regard to form alone, it could be said that both series match Empson's definition of the pastoral: they put the complex into the simple.[31] Only the *Frog and Toad* series, however, deals with the essence of pastoral—felicitous space, be it home or meadow.

George and Martha each have their own home as do Frog and Toad, but their homes are simply one of several settings and far from integral to either plot or characterization. George and Martha are city folk and live smack in the middle of the "clank of the world." Place is not as significant as action. If George and Martha were to make a list of things to do, it would include telephones, microscopes, movies, photographs, amusement parks, cement sidewalks, and all the tertiary characters and events connected with such items. They are as busy as they are big.

George and Martha are also more often involved in conflicts based on the building and maintenance of a friendship, that is, honesty, privacy, hurt feelings, and empathy. For Marshall, friendship is a subject. For Lobel, it is a primary part of the pastoral setting.

These contrasts are also reflected in their respective illustrations. Size or species alone creates a significant difference in tone. Visually Frog and Toad are common creatures. Decidedly members of a nonheroic class, they are naturally pastoral.[32] They live close to the earth, sometimes hidden by it, but forever vulnerable. Their only method of protection is to hide or flee. Though anthropomorphized, Lobel keeps their personalities, environment, and atmosphere on a plane parallel to their biological reality.

Marshall's George and Martha, however, derive much of their humor from their images's sharp contrasts with their actions and reality. The action itself may not be comic, for example, dancing ballet or leaping after an errant jumping bean, but the image of a hippo doing it *is*. Just as they are forever working through the clashes in their relationship, George and Martha's world is visually a constant clash. They are exotic animals in a city. They wear "noisy" clothes, and even in a hippo-sized room, they seem out of place. Easily able to squash anything in their way, they do not so much evoke laughter through the reader's recognition of an emotional situation as do Frog and Toad, but rather spark laughter itself at their incongruities.

Grahame and Potter

It is impossible to discuss Frog and Toad without also referring to both Kenneth Grahame and Beatrix Potter. Lobel's work has been frequently compared to theirs and fits well midway between the two. Knowledge of his own experience with their work is limited. Though he did not view *The Wind in the Willows* as a children's book, Lobel remembered reading it in high school and thought it "a lovely book"[33] and certainly an influence on his work.[34] Potter is one of a handful of twentieth-century illustrators of whom he spoke admiringly—"Beatrix Potter, for one, obviously."[35] Her books are not among the few titles he remembered from the many he read as a child, but it is likely he encountered at least some of her books during high school in the late forties and early fifties. Though not yet thinking of a career in picture books, he became fascinated by them as an art form and checked out stacks of them from the library.

Lobel's most immediate connection with Grahame and Potter is his pastoral setting and use of clothed animals. By turn, he is closer to one than the other. Frog and Toad remain dressed (except, of course, Frog when swimming) as do Mole and Ratty. Different Potter characters are dressed all of the time, some of the time, or never. Yet, Lobel is closer to Potter in keeping his "human-animals" in character with their animal nature (i.e., frowning-burrowing Toad and on-the-go Frog). At the same time, like Grahame's crew, Frog and Toad stick to civilized human food such as tea, cookies, ice cream, and sandwiches with mustard. Had Frog and Toad ever served up, Jeremy Fisher-style, a tray of butterfly sandwiches, the earthy green buddies would have suddenly seemed cute.

Unlike Grahame and Potter, however, Lobel never clouds the boundaries of proportion or animal fantasy by including humans. The literary worlds of Grahame and Potter exist within the human world. Even if no humans appear, Potter's animal characters often use supplies such as acorn cups and dollhouse dishes. In contrast, Frog and Toad do not so much share our human world as inhabit their own which is parallel to ours. Except for their species, there is nothing "less than human" about them. Nor is there any sense of "back then" with Frog and Toad. For that, there must be urban elements and nonpastoral characters to stress the contrast. Grahame and Potter have villages filled with humans counting time. Frog and Toad, alone in their world, exist in Arcadia's perpetual noon and outside of time and history.

With time suspended for Frog and Toad, so are their ages. Like Mole and Ratty to a lesser degree (the appearance of children such as Portly Otter implies some aging), Frog and Toad are child substitutes forever in their eleventh year. They are forever free of adult burdens related to family, work, and sex. Though she alludes on occasion to magical worlds (i.e., *Mrs. Tiggy-Winkle*), Potter's eye is always on the clock. All of her characters will enter adulthood if they haven't already.

These pastoral aspects of time reveal the significant differences between Potter and *Frog and Toad* stories, once one looks beyond a shared attentiveness to detail, home, and zoology. The *Frog and Toad* narratives are clearly vignettes or idylls—little pictures. They are glimpses rather than time passed. Potter's tales though brief are fully plotted stories with passing time. They contain overt danger, battles with outsiders, and the required resolutions such adventures bring.

Potter's voice as storyteller is always present (at times literally so as in *The Tale of Benjamin Bunny*) and matches the richness and awareness of style that fill her illustrations. She can speak with elegant politeness as in *The Roly-Poly Pudding*: "But I am persuaded that the knots would have proved indigestible, whatever you may urge to the contrary"[36] or with polite bluntness as in *The Tale of Peter Rabbit*: "Father had an accident there; he was put in a pie by Mrs. McGregor."[37]

Lobel's presence does not exist in the *Frog and Toad* stories, at all. In true pastoral style *Frog and Toad* work as dramatic dialogues rather than as stories told. And, as the stories' literary genre (idyll) defines their range of content and perspective, Frog and Toad know none of the dangers of Potter's world. Lobel has no need nor desire for Potter's gentleman farmer tone regarding the pains of life. When their dialogue, on occasion, *is* blunt, it doesn't reflect the teller's perspective on events in the story, but rather the intimacy, honesty, and longevity of their friendship. They need few words. When Toad in "The Dream" wakes up after his nightmare and announces with great relief: "Frog . . . ? I am so glad / that you came over." Frog simply states the obvious and without judgment: "I always do" (*FTT,* 63).

Frog may have little to say compared to Potter's characters (and Toad even less), but thanks to Lobel's gifted "plain writing" what they do say is said with finesse and through context made rich in content. When Toad wakes up in "The Dream" from his nightmare of a shrinking Frog and eagerly asks if Frog is his own right size, Frog does not quibble about the question or condescend by saying, "of course." He treats the question as a valid one (which it is in Toad's eyes) and answers "I think so" (*FTT,* 63), which still leaves him room to correct himself should he find he is mistaken. In a later story, "Christmas Eve," Toad's mind races with disastrous reasons as to why Frog is late. When he finally finds him safe and not at the bottom of a well or lost in the woods, Toad asks: "You are not being eaten by a big animal?" (*FTAY*, 63). Again Frog answers simply, honestly, and with respect for the question, "No." And then to show that the question could be valid, he adds in the style of a true friend and gentleman who checks every detail: "Not at all" (*FTAY*, 63).

Distinctly different in style, both Potter and Lobel support their stories' forms and content through their voices, she as the whalebone and taffeta raconteur come to tea and he as the joyful flute player in the shade of the tree.

Though similar in overall tone and setting to Mole and Ratty, Frog and Toad also differ from them in significant ways. Both *The Wind in the Willows* and the *Frog and Toad* books celebrate friendship between male characters, but while Grahame's approach is primarily escapist and misogynist, Lobel's is one of unity. Grahame often spoke against women as angrily as he spoke against the lower class and growing up. "'O, I have girls,' said Toad when posing as a washerwoman. 'But you know what *girls* are, ma'am! Nasty little hussies, that's what *I* call 'em!'"[38] It is as if he included minor female characters merely so that he could discount them in front of his readers.

Focusing on only two friends, rather than an entire gentleman's club, as Grahame did, Lobel is more interested in the nature of their personal relationship than in the society that surrounds and/or defines them. By excluding everyone except Frog and Toad, Lobel in effect excludes no one.

That Frog and Toad are both male is in keeping with the pastoral tradition of shepherd-shepherd friendship,[39] but it becomes even more Arcadian when read by twentieth-century eyes concerned with gender equality. No one has explained it more clearly than Christopher Bram in his 1981 essay, "Little Green Buddies":

> Simply by changing pronouns, he could have made his friends female, or one female and the other male. Society expects its females to be sharply conscious of each move

in the intricate business of their friendships, but expects its males, even as children, to be above such attention to emotional detail. By making both of his friends members of the "strong" gender, Lobel goes against convention. He never draws attention to this revolt. Lobel presents his amphibians' attention to details as something natural and unbounded by gender, which it is. Not only do Frog and Toad live in a fulfilled dream of loyalty and kindness, they live in a world that approaches a true sexual democracy.[40]

Through instinctive selection of form, setting, theme, character, voice, and gender, Lobel created a thoroughly Arcadian experience for his readers. And, as "the artist embodies in himself the attitude of the perceiver while he works,"[41] Lobel continually experiences the book-bound felicitous space he had treasured since childhood and longed to share. "Frog and Toad belong to no one," he said many times in many ways, "but they belong to everyone, every sector: rich children, poor children, white children, black children. Everybody can relate to Frog and Toad because they don't exist in this world."[42]

6

A Room Full of Windows

... the animals are mouthpieces for different aspects of myself.[1]

Though Lobel's Caldecott Medal book *Fables* (1980) was not conceived or published until the late seventies, almost everything he had written up to that point had been related to the fable in some degree, be it in tone, form, or use of animal characters. *Lucille* (1964), his first "I Can Read" text, could have easily concluded with the same moral Lobel assigned "The Hen and the Apple Tree" in *Fables:* "It is always difficult to pose as something that one is not" (*F,* 11). From their first volume in 1970, Frog and Toad lived in the fable's world of anthropomorphic stories that center on human behavior distilled to its essence. Even without morals, *Frog and Toad* clearly offered insight into the shared human condition by showing readers themselves.

With most historians of the fable[2] regarding the fable as poetry, hence song, *Fables* is a book well suited to the pastoral world of Lobel's work. All of his earlier characters, especially Frog and Toad, can easily be imagined reading *Fables*. Director John Matthews even had Toad read "The Frogs at the Rainbow's End" from *Fables* to his frightened seeds in the wonderful Churchill film version of *Frog and Toad Together*.

Still, even taken separately from the *Frog and Toad* series and his other pastoral work, *Fables* and the fable genre in general are pastoral in many ways, particularly in their relationship to audience. As Lobel well understood, all readers can enter the stories on an equal level by entering through the animal characters. King and peasant, adult and child are equals for the length of the fable, for it appeals equally to both groups. And with everyone able to enter, everyone exists in the genre's glass house, leaving no one on the outside free to throw stones.

The fable also exists in a timeless state, much like the pastoral. Though anthropomorphized, the animals in fables have no genuine sense of place and maintain their animal lack of time or history. Unaware of the past and future, they will forever possess their foibles and repeat foolish behaviors. Things happen *to* them (much like classic noodleheads or protagonists in modern short stories) but they most often remain unaware or inactive. Created as glimpses into behavior, fable characters cannot evolve, as their stories have no plot.

Like all stories and anecdotes, fables are naturally told in the past tense as singular incidents. But even as they are being told or read, the audience knows that the fable is perpetual. The story, that element of human behavior, has actually happened many times and will continue to happen. Even Lobel's fables that do hint at growth and conclude with a more positive moral maintain the genre's sense of perpetuity. Dancing camels must forever learn to satisfy themselves, and mice children will be making journeys to the seashore as long as the world exists.

If one looks by analogy at Lobel's "I Can Read" texts as excellent short stories (which they are), *Fables,* at the time of its publication, was seen as his first novel. *Fables* was literally bigger, brighter, and larger than anything he had done to date. And for the first time he labeled his stories as fables. Both the expectation awaiting such a "major" work by an artist of stature and the fact that the term *fable* has become as mercurial and territorial as the term *pastoral* contributed to extremes in reviews of the book.

The *New Yorker*[3] and *Newsweek* each published glowing full-page reviews that included interviews with Lobel. The latter praised him as "an Aesop for our time" and "at once more humane and more lighthearted than Aesop."[4] Paul Heins, in *Horn Book,* pronounced Lobel's fables as having "an original flavor" and "deceptively ingenious narrative developments frequently embellished with preposterous situations and completed with a moral smacking of deliberately gleeful cynicism."[5]

In contrast, *Kirkus Reviews* found *Fables* flat and predictable without "a jot of wit, wisdom, style, or originality."[6] *School Library Journal's* Patricia Dooley felt many of the narratives were weak and "defective in that their 'morals' are unclear until stated."[7] Quality of narratives aside, the basis of her review exists in direct opposition to critic Richard Tobias's view that "both the riddle and the fable are the oldest forms of writing . . . and both demand that the reader be surprised by their resolution or their moral."[8]

Two of the most extreme responses came from education publications and are indicative of reviewer preconceptions regarding both the fable and Lobel's relationship to it. In the *Times Educational Supplement* (London) Naomi Lewis paired Lobel's *Fables* with a new edition of Aesop. "The 20 [*sic*] original fables . . . seem at first glance very much of the Aesop kind; but Lobel thinks a stage further. Where Aesop inclines to the heavy-pragmatic, Lobel can show a grain of imagination; you could even call it poetry."[9] Ruth Stein of *Language Arts* violently disagreed. "The twenty fables about an array of animal characters are more short stories than succinct observations on human foibles. The italicized morals seem less pointed lessons than fortune cookie comments or daily astrological forecasts. There was little originality or amusement. Frankly, I'll stick with Frog and Toad."[10] Clearly, as Aesop states at the conclusion of "The Father and his Two Daughters," "You can't please everybody."[11]

In some ways Lobel's own genre-stretching work with the *Frog and Toad* books and even *Owl at Home* and *Grasshopper on the Road* created part of the begrudging remarks toward *Fables*. Using dialogue rather than narration and the same characters in each tale, Lobel had been able to give each Frog and Toad fable an emotional depth and individuality beyond that of the traditional fable. There was no way he could achieve the same aggregate tone, depth, and characterization of the *Frog and Toad* volumes in the singular tales of *Fables,* no matter how well he wrote them.

Calling this collection of tales "fables" also brought immediate and very subjective comparisons to Aesop. The fables of Aesop and their morals are accepted as age-old wisdom and the shared experience of the masses, no matter how many times they are retold. A contemporary writer, however, ending a new fable with one of Aesop's morals (or one written in the same tone) is easily rejected as a rather pompous pusher of clichés. Taken alone, the maxims *are* clichés, as are most proverbs. The task of the fable writer rests in finding new ways to reveal the same behavior so that the truth within the cliché will seem suddenly fresh again.

The primary approaches the twentieth-century fabulist can take are 1) reducing the form to even greater simplicity or 2) making use of the fable form and formality and innate sense of humor. Leo Lionni has explored the greater-simplicity approach without forfeiting depth in *Inch by Inch* (1960) and *Swimmy* (1963). Thurber's *Fables of Our Time* (1940) published for adults remains the premiere parody of the genre, while still creating viable new fables through ironic humor. *Fables You Shouldn't Pay Any Attention To* (1978) by Heide and Van Clief are tales told in complete contrast to tradition with concluding lines such as "I'm glad I was selfish, it pays."[12] It is only the book's title that turns the tales into true fables of humorous instruction.

Studying the ways in which folk literature appears in contemporary literature, William Jansen delineated three levels: 1) style—sounds, motifs, and images; 2) material—as springboard for individual fiction; and 3) performance/interpretation—just as an actor offers his version of a particular role.[13] *Fables,* at one time or another, falls into all three categories. Dividing and labeling Lobel's twenty fables would serve little purpose, but exploring how many reflect Jansen's thesis may, as a fable should, help one see the topic at hand more clearly than before.

Style

Lobel used animals for his characters in true fable tradition, but in a slightly different manner. As he did with Frog and Toad, he extended visual characteristics to characterization. Only a few characters are consistent with their natural predatory behaviors, yet all of his selections are well suited to their stories. One's general perception of a crocodile is exactly that of "The Crocodile in the Bedroom," a green animal forever lying still. Dogs are often poor street creatures as in "The Poor Old Dog." Camels are famous for their awkward gait. Kangaroos are forever fidgety and poorly behaved. Bears are never seen as graceful or stylish, and the rhino is most often viewed standing in a pose that begs to be noticed. Any animal larger than a mouse would have detracted from the power of "The Mouse at the Seashore." On occasion Lobel even worked against type or perception as with "The Elephant and His Son," in which the animal who never forgets is completely unaware of current events. Fables by their very nature employ animals as safely furred mirrors, but are traditionally drawn as naturalistic animals. Lobel, as few others have done save his "teachers," J. J. Grandville and Charles Bennett (illustrators of acclaimed nineteenth-century editions of Aesop), clothed his animals, giving visual acknowledgment of their connection to the reader's world.

Material

After studying Aesop's fables for several months before starting on his own, Lobel very naturally included many motifs and characters as material for his own. Several of his fables seem to be direct, though perhaps unconscious, responses to specific tales. "The Camel Dances" and "The Ostrich in Love" are certainly descendants of "The Monkey and the Camel" and "Lion in Love," but far gentler and empathetic in tone.

Aesop's camel is a pseudocritic who, after misunderstanding the value and quality of a comic performance, brags that he can do better, meaning more seriously. When he does *his* awkward dance, he is quickly booed by others. Both villain and victim, Aesop's camel receives a harsh moral: "Stretch your arm no further than your sleeve will reach."[14] Lobel's camel, however, dances not to criticize another, but because she loves it and practices for months. "Her feet were blistered, and her body ached with fatigue, but not once did she think of stopping" (*F*, 22). Lobel's camel also has critics who are as cruel as those in Aesop, yet Camel has no need of challenging them. Once her audience has laughed and left, Camel tells herself, "I have worked hard. There can be no doubt that I am a splendid dancer. I will dance and dance just for myself." Lobel's moral is: "Satisfaction will come to those who please themselves" (*F*, 22). By skillfully leaving out an objective assessment of Camel's dancing, he adds resonance to his moral. It may be that she was a good dancer, and that the critics were wrong. It may also be true that she was a bad dancer, but the quality doesn't matter as long as she enjoys her creativity and pleases herself.

Aesop's Lion and Lobel's Ostrich are both in love and both lose their beloved. Lion is too gullible; Ostrich too shy. Lion gives up his claws and teeth for love and is then beaten by his beloved's human father. Ostrich, in contrast, is his own worst enemy and the only barrier to a chance to be with his beloved. He has no emotional claws or teeth. He spends a week writing songs and poems for her, but never shares them with her. Still too shy to even introduce himself at the end of the week, Ostrich consoles himself by deciding it was still a week well spent. Lobel's moral "Love can be its own reward" is certainly a basic truth, yet his use of Ostrich evokes further thought. Was it, if archetypal Ostrich had his head and bravery stuck in the sand, truly a week well spent? Is Ostrich celebrating the joy one feels when loving another or merely consoling himself like a fox over sour grapes and dismissing his timidity and failure? It is such resonances that give Lobel's best fables their depth and poetry.

"The Pelican and the Crane" is clearly a cousin tale to Aesop's "The Fox and the Stork." The differences between the two point to Lobel's manner of using Aesop as a springboard, making such elements his own. As with "The Camel Dances" and "Ostrich in Love," Lobel's tale of dining etiquette is based on individual behaviors rather than confrontation. Rather than pitting one character against the other, Lobel's Pelican is his own worst enemy. While visiting Crane, Pelican laments never being invited to dinner parties, all the while making a disgusting mess of his food. Lobel concludes: "When one is a social failure, the reasons are as clear as day" (*F*, 35)—except, that is, to the failure himself.

"The Hen and the Apple Tree" is yet another Lobelian branch off Aesop's tree and could have concluded with one of several Aesopian morals: "He who is once deceived is doubly cautious," "Beware of the insincere friend," "The best liars often get caught in their own lies," or "Clothes may disguise a fool, but his words will give him away."[15] Instead, Lobel concludes with one of his work's primary themes: "It is always difficult to pose as something that one is not" (*F*, 11). But this time the maxim applies to the villain rather than a troubled hero. Posing as an apple tree, Wolf tries to seduce Hen into leaving her house for his pastoral shade. This hen, however, is no chicken-little. She observes the "tree" carefully and sets up her trap by politely expressing her disbelief over what trees do. To each statement Wolf quickly answers "This tree does." Once the pattern is established, Hen puts out her bait in the form of an innocent statement: "I have heard that some of you trees lose all your leaves at this time of year" (*F*, 11). Eager to prove his "treeness" Wolf shakes loose his leaves thus exposing himself. "The Hen was not surprised to see a large Wolf in the place where an apple tree had been standing just a moment before" (*F*, 11). Not at all. Hen had savored, as did the reader, every minute of her outsmarting Wolf. And, because she was always in control of the situation, one begins to feel empathy for Wolf. He is not, in the end, so much a villain as a schlemiel trying to be a villain.

Performance

Coming as he did to *Fables* after deciding he could not retell and illustrate Aesop as suggested by editors at Harper & Row, Lobel's entire set of fables can be viewed as his interpretation or performance of the fable genre. His exist as a response to what he liked and disliked about Aesop's tales and as his personal extension of the genre after years of Frog and Toad stories. As discussed above, Lobel employed various motifs, images, and tales, recasting them in his own way, but his performance is most distinctive in regard to voice and use of morals.

With the fable form so connected with Aesop, the fables associated with his name are often assumed to be the only proper ones, just as all myths are assumed to adhere to the structure and tone of Greek myths. Characteristics usually assigned to Aesop's fables quickly go beyond genre (a brief metaphoric tale that highlights a human foible and thereby instructs in a pleasing or humorous manner) to voice (a wagging finger and ironic smugness). Far from being a literary sage, Aesop, as depicted in folktales about him,[16] was more a trickster thoroughly in control of the powers that be and admired by everyone but those in power. Even when humorous, Aesop's voice remains sharp and combative, the antithesis of Lobel's pastoral nonsense.

Just as he did in his "I Can Read" texts, Lobel tells in *Fables* of absurdities or foibles taken to absurd extremes. The incongruity of this with the calm pastoral manner of "plain writing" contributed greatly to the nonsense and humor of the earlier stories. With *Fables* the incongruity has been increased through a tongue-in-cheek use of elegant language and perspective. Danger may be lurking around the corner and social codes torn to shreds, but Lobel speaks with a Victorian's propriety and distance. It is as if Sir John Gielgud is playing a butler in Times Square, believing everything will be just fine if only good posture and correct grammar can be maintained. The crocodile doesn't just run back to his bedroom, he rushes back in "a state of great distress" (*F,* 2). Camel's critics don't simply laugh at her dancing. They announce with noses in the air that she is "lumpy and humpy. You are baggy and bumpy" (*F,* 22). And Hippopotamus wants a truly lip-smacking "*bathtub* of bean soup, a *bucket* of Brussels sprouts, and a *mountain* of mashed potatoes" (*F,* 38). Throughout, *Fables* is laced with Lobel's playful sense of language and sound. And his "Victorian" voice combined with his sense of self-parody comes to function as his beloved comic element of false dignity exposed.

The overriding differences from Aesop in Lobel's *Fables* are selection and use of morals. As reflected in the disparate reviews of *Fables,* the debate over whether or not to use a moral to close fables and, if so, in what manner is long and varied. While some feel the moral should be a surprise or at least an extension, Joseph Jacobs believed: "Either your fable makes its point [alone] or it does not."[17] At one point in history, popular opinion held that the moral should begin the fable. In hoping to bypass what he saw as Aesop's dry didacticism, Lobel initially planned to have no morals with his fables. Still, the current expectation is to end with a moral. "If a fable is a fable," he decided, "it must have a moral. It's like dropping the other shoe. You have the story and then—pomf!—you have to have that little kicker."[18]

Lobel's use of "kickers" remained true to his pastoral sense of unity through revelation of shared condition. Rather than Aesop's wagging finger saying "Look at you," Lobel wrote with a nodding smile saying "Will you look at *us.*" "The characters in the fables," he told *Instructor,* "may be self-aggrandizing or self-deprecating but they are part of me. And supposedly, since I'm a regular average human being, people will recognize themselves, too, and find a universal meaning."[19]

As often as not Lobel's morals are affirmations of wise behavior (i.e., "Satisfaction will come to those who please themselves") or neutral observations (i.e., "When one is a social failure, the reasons are as clear as day") as opposed to exposures of foolish actions. Although many of Aesop's morals are neutral observations, Lobel had none of Aesop's biting judgments such as "The greedy who want more lose all" or "The smaller the mind the greater the conceit."[20]

Even with morals included as the "dropping of the other shoe," or closure, Lobel's fables are more like the open-ended Frog and Toad stories than is immediately apparent. Seeing the moral as part of the fable's form, Lobel also made it a part of his interpretive performance. "Some of my morals are a bit facetious."[21]. Others are slightly "impish."[22] In Lobel's hands some of the concluding morals confirm the narrative, some give a surprise twist, and some are a teasing back-flip on the narrative. With this approach his morals function not so much as "kickers" themselves, but as a doctor's rubber mallet that causes the reader to respond with a mental kicker—a poststory reflection—that gives both the tale and the moral an added twist and depth. These "sub-morals," as Marie Winn called them in her review in the *New York Times Book Review,*[23] allow the reader more involvement than traditional or Aesopian fables, for they call out for the reader's contribution, and in doing so, once again establish the pastoral equality between teller and audience.

As with other tales discussed above, it is the reader's juxtaposing of moral to narrative that creates the concluding insight and unwritten moral. Rather than narrative and moral being a monologue and summary, it is as if the two are in a dialogue in *Fables.* Two fine examples of this are "The Lobster and the Crab" and "The Young Rooster." "The Lobster and the Crab" moves briskly through exciting events to its moral: "Even the taking of small risks will add excitement to life" (*F,* 8). Taken alone, the moral is true and direct, yet as one lets it refract against the story, it becomes an exercise in absurdity. The exciting risk and boat crash at sea happen to two sea creatures. Their excitement and risk are based entirely on perception rather than factual danger. It is laughable, yet this contradiction is the true core of Lobel's fable and gives additional depth to his moral. No matter what the outer reality of circumstances, the taking of risks is based entirely within the risk-taker's mind and *is* invigorating whatever the risk.

"The Young Rooster" is equally multilayered. Initially chided by barnyard critics for his weak crowing, young rooster is also chided for being too loud once he improves and crows "the loudest crow that was ever crowed since the beginning of roosters" (*F,* 37). Lobel's moral, "A first failure may prepare the way for later success" (*F,* 37), is true and assuring in its most direct interpretation, but holds even more. When viewed as a responding line in a dialogue, it also establishes that the young rooster's critics have nothing to do with his personal satisfaction in growth or success in a job well done. He has succeeded whether they welcome his improvement or not.

Rather than merely reproducing what had gone before or what was expected, Lobel, like the young rooster, extended his form to perhaps more than many critics could appreciate. First, with characterization in the *Frog and Toad* books and then with pastoral nonsense and dialogue between story and moral in *Fables,* he used what existed as seed to create new hybrids of the fable, which were at once old and new. These hybrids may not be, nor do they need to be everyone's favorite, but they are honest and invigorating additions to the genre.

Just as the tales themselves were his largest written work to date, the illustrations in *Fables* were simply more in every way than any he had done before. Reaction again ran the gamut from the book's being honored with the 1981 Caldecott Medal to critic Barbara Bader's declaring the illustrations boring.[24] As with the texts, they are an acknowledgment of a genre different from much of his earlier work and at the same time still related.

Like his other books of the seventies, Lobel illustrated *Fables*'s characters in full dress. The style and setting, however, is Victorian rather than pastoral, and that change initiated others. The small visual vignettes in soft colors and shapes used in the *Frog and Toad* books would have all but disappeared next to the directness and self-awareness of Lobel's formalized fables. Done instead in a large format with a lushness of color, texture, and line, Lobel's images for *Fables* balance both the style and emotional weight of his prose. The heightened visual style is a direct echo of Lobel's proper voice in the face of disaster. The incongruity of rich style and absurd content extends the humor of false dignity exposed. When the illustrations depict a positive behavior as in "The Camel Dances" and "The Mouse at the Seashore," the richness of color and visual depth give resonance to the characters' joy.

Reduced to a single image per story, the illustrations in *Fables* also become more emblematic than narrative. Like movie posters, they must refer to the story in a way that sparks interest without giving the action away and yet, in the end, work in one's memory as a coherent symbol for the entire fable. Particularly effective are the images for "The Hen and the Apple Tree," "The Bear and the Crow," "The Elephant and his Son," and "The Mouse at the Seashore." Each illustration stems from a different point in its respective narrative, yet each captures a key moment of emotion.

While large and bold in format, *Fables* still evokes a degree of Lobel's "Come-gather-round" manner of illustration and book design. He had long appreciated Lear's edition of limericks, which featured one verse and image per page, and Charles Bennett's edition of Aesop's fables, which featured the fable on one page and its illustration on the other. Though he has stated that he borrowed Bennett's format,[25] it is just as likely, knowing he had long used framing, that he would have done so on his own and that it was that preference that drew him to Lear and Bennett. It is this sense of framing with solid space surrounding the full-color image that acknowledges the reader and says "Come-gather-round." Like Matisse's paintings of windows that act as a passageway between two worlds, Lobel's design of *Fables* establishes the simultaneity of two worlds, in this case those of the reader and of the fable. Visually he connects the two worlds just as the reader does in his thoughts, with the white frame acting as a wall in the reader's room and the illustration existing as the parallel world viewed through the window. And as with all windows when approached from the right perspective, these, like the fables themselves, become reflecting mirrors of the reader's own world.

7

Tales for Sleep and Safety

I'm partial to cozy books.[1]

Between the first and final *Frog and Toad* volumes Lobel wrote two "I Can Read" anthologies, *Mouse Tales* (1972) and *Mouse Soup* (1977). Both are stories within a framing story. Both are filled with the celebration of incongruities, and both share Lobel's perspective of story and nonsense as Arcadian or pastoral interludes.

Pappa Mouse tells seven comic tales as a way of calming his seven little mouse boys to sleep. All seven tales attest to Lobel's knack of knowing when a story is working dramatically. "I wrote lots and lots and lots of them and I threw away lots and lots."[2] The stories he kept are so tightly written, they shine and move with a lively beat.

"The Journey" and "The Bath" are fresh examples of reductio ad absurdum. On his way to visit his mother a mouse child wears out a car, then skates, then boots, then sneakers, then feet! But not to worry. He simply gets a new pair of feet from a mad scientist-looking salesman along the road *and* a matter-of-fact compliment on them from his mother. "The Bath" begins with a mouse blithely fulfilling every child's fantasy of letting the bath water run till it overflows. Oblivious to the disaster he is creating, mouse keeps scrubbing away as the entire village floods, then he dries off and falls asleep without a care.

"Clouds" and "The Mouse and the Winds" both employ familiar plots, but Lobel successfully adds a fresh twist. As in many other picture books, the mouse child in "Clouds" learns to see pictures in the clouds by using his imagination. Lobel weaves in a blend of the absurd and darker sides. Left alone, mouse child's imagination runs away from him and he sees a terrifying cat in the clouds. In reassuring him that it was just a cloud in the sky like all the other images, his mother respects the reality of his emotions and never implies his fears were wrong or silly. Still, it was a powerful experience for the mouse child, and Lobel doesn't dismiss it any more than mouse's mother did. Lobel concludes with the child feeling better, but "he did not look up at the sky for the rest of the afternoon."[3]

In "The Mouse and the Winds" it is nature that gets carried away and carries away the characters. It is at once a predecessor to *Grasshopper on the Road*'s picaresque hero and a cumulative nonsense story. Though there may be concern as the winds rearrange a growing list of things including mountains and homes, mouse never panics because he feels joy in the adventure of change.

The other three tales are variations on themes explored in earlier books. "The Well" is a tale with a comic switch, in which the mouse cannot get *her* wishes for gifts from the wishing well until after she thinks on her own of a gift to give the well. Here the gift is a pillow tossed down the well so that the well won't feel pain as coins are thrown in for wishes. As Lobel showed in the *Frog and Toad* series, giving brings its own gift.

The coexistence of differences, which runs as a primary thread throughout the *Frog and Toad* books, indeed through all of Lobel's work, is beautifully distilled in "Very Tall Mouse and Very Short Mouse." Being so different in size, the two mice literally have different perspectives on the world (i.e., birds-bugs, roof-cellar, raindrops-puddles), but both perspectives are valid or true. And because the mice's friendship allows them to accept their differences, they are both able to see the rainbow, which has long been a symbol of hope and peace.

Taken as metaphor, "The Old Mouse" can be seen as the essence of Lobel's work, for he believed "we laugh at incongruity and we laugh at lack of dignity. If a man's pants fall down everybody laughs, children, adults."[4] In this tale, pants literally drop. A crotchety old mouse's pants fall down. The children laugh. His wife says he looks silly and gives him a Punch-and-Judy hit on the head. With his dignity, or rather his artificial dignity, gone and his humanness/mouseness exposed, the old mouse cries. Now that he is vulnerable and approachable, the children console him and give him chewing gum to keep up his pants. The absurdity gives way to a sense of equality between child and adult. Lobel's statement on the story in the *Lion and the Unicorn* reflects the spirit behind his comedy of foibles revealed as well as comedy's vital role in creating Arcadia. "This very pompous, unpleasant person was reduced to something comical, and indeed, that's when children were able to relate to him and they did and they helped him and he began to love them."[5]

Lobel's approach is a rephrasing of Frye's theory that the "theme of the comic is the integration of society."[6] With foibles revealed, says Lobel through his stories, we are all made vulnerable. We are then all able to relate to one another as equals and, in turn, help and love one another. This is not because no differences or flaws exist, but because they do and are shared by everyone.

While Lobel's pastoral sensibilities shaped his humor, his humor kept his pastoral world strong and alive. His use of surprise or back-flip conclusions in *Mouse Tales* echoes Theocritus' use of the surprise punch line to "pump energy and lustiness [vigor] back into a bower."[7]

Mouse Soup takes the value of story beyond a warm nighttime ritual into the realm of literally saving one's life. "I always wanted to do something with Scheherazade, but with kids I can't go on for 1001 nights and have a seduction. So, I turned to mice. They're small and vulnerable, and children seem to identify with them."[8]

Not only does the telling of stories keep Mouse alive à la Scheherazade and uneaten by Weasel, the stories mouse tells are completely Lobel—"genial, artless nonsense."[9]

At the moment Mouse is captured by Weasel he is experiencing the pastoral interlude of reading beneath a shady tree, much as Lobel remembers doing as a child.[10] And, as soon as the ordeal is over, mouse "hurried / to his safe home. / He lit the fire, / he ate his supper, / and he finished / reading his book."[11] Mouse's ongoing reading clearly gave him the preparation for saving himself by telling stories. Mouse also reflects Lobel's and Owl's *(Owl at Home)* love of objects. Weasel can't put the stories in the soup, but he can, advises Mouse, put the objects of each tale (beehive, mud, stones, and crickets) in the soup because they hold the stories.

With "Two Large Stones" and "The Thorn Bush" Lobel explores again his theme of one's perceptions creating one's truest reality or Arcadia. When a bird tells the two stones that the other side of the hill is (through its perspective) "a wonderful sight" with towns, castles, mountains, and valleys, the stones' next hundred years are very sad. They mourn all that they will never see. Then, when a mouse (within Lobel's world mice are always more nurturing than birds) tells the two stones that the other side of the hill is (through its perspective) "a wonderful sight" with earth, stones, grass, and flowers, just like *their* side of the hill, the stones know they will be happy forever. Lobel's two stones are easily duped cousins of the Chelmites of Yiddish lore who, on a journey, after unknowingly turning around, think they have found a village just like their own when in fact it *is* their own village. It is a noodlehead tale on the surface, yet in Lobel's hands the fact that their happiness is based on what they imagine the world to be exists as a poetic residue long after the laughter has faded. The key to whether or not their world is Arcadian is clearly based on what they chose to believe, regardless of literal situation.

Mouse's final story, "The Thorn Bush," also deals with the joy of unique perception and the celebration of incongruity. An old lady mouse is not upset because a thorn bush had suddenly started growing out of her stuffed chair. She is upset because it is wilting. Accepting the initial nonsense, the old lady and the policeman can proceed to figure out that the thorn bush is thirsty, water it, and celebrate its large rose blooms. "You have made / my house beautiful!" exclaims the lady mouse: "She kissed the policeman / and gave him a big bunch / of roses to take home" (51). By accepting/watering her nonsense—the thorn bush growing in her armchair and *her* acceptance of that nonsense—the policeman helped a garden grow. He entered her world of nonsense and left refreshed.

Deliberate or not, the design of both *Mouse Tales* and *Mouse Soup* reflects how stories bring focus and structure to our lives. While the outer stories or stories of the stories in both books are illustrated with visual vignettes that float free on the page, the stories told by the mice characters are illustrated (for the most part) by framed images. Each page of a story Mouse tells is also framed near trim size, the text and image held within. Even when filled with absurdities, stories are more ordered than life—life being the forest, story the garden.

Mouse Tales and *Mouse Soup* are the epitome of Lobel's perception of nonsense humor as the primary song of Arcadia. As he tells his tales of absurdity, Lobel echoes the burlesque and comic songs of Victorian England in laughing for laughter's sake rather than as social critique. In doing so, he gives his literary mice and human readers the same sense of temporary Arcadia or "holiday from judgment"[12] that Victorian humorists gave their readers. The nonsensical content of Pappa Mouse's tales in *Mouse Tales* and of Mouse's book and tales in *Mouse Soup* is in the end as pastoral in evocation as the settings in which the tales are told and read. Both volumes, though unassuming in form and appearance, are prime examples of the duality that Lobel felt marked the work of those author-artists he most admired: "the best ones are able to make them delightful on one level, but that's just the whipped cream on top. Underneath there is something [*sic*] much more."[13]

8

The Man Inside the Animal Suit

> The children don't know, but the truth of the story,
> whatever gives it validity, is its truth to me, as an
> adult.[1]

With *Owl at Home* (1975), *Grasshopper on the Road* (1978), and *Uncle Elephant* (1981) Lobel created three characters as vividly defined by their individuality as Frog and Toad are by their friendship. While each is unique, all three are characters of reverie and dramatize Lobel's belief in what could be called a pastoral of attitude. For Lobel and these three creatures Arcadia is the manner in which one sees the world. As Nancy Willard writes of object-poet Francis Ponge, these characters "know that to say the world is absurd means only that it cannot be mapped by human reason. The real triumph of reason is to recognize this."[2] Doing so, they are able to celebrate life's continual incongruities and live in their own Arcadias. Together the three volumes form a metaphoric autobiography of Lobel.

As one who invites the winter indoors, is frightened by his own feet, tries to be in two places at once, and thinks the moon is following him home, Owl of *Owl at Home* is a first-class resident of the fool's village of Chelm. Lobel himself described Owl as a "complete psychotic . . . [with] no sense of gravity to his thinking."[3] Yet the laughter Owl evokes is not that toward one deemed lesser. He does not exist outside reality, but rather deeply within it. Like Charlie Chaplin (whose films Lobel admired), Owl is an archetype or a heightened version of a certain kind of person. In this case, it is Lobel's obsessiveness stretched to the utmost extreme. As with all of Lobel's fable-fiction, when one laughs at Owl's behavior, he is really accepting and laughing at the Owl within himself. And, in this laughter, a pastoral moment for one's self is made.

With "The Guest" Lobel creates a comic disaster that is the reverse of *The Man Who Took the Indoors Out,* published the previous year. Rather than taking the indoors out, Owl brings the outdoors—winter—indoors. It is an act of foolish kindness that destroys his pastoral home of food, flowers, fireplace, and books, just as surely as the reciprocal change destroyed the same for Bellwood Bouse. Finally accepting the coexisting differences between the indoors and outdoors, Owl is able to return to his fireplace and food.

"Strange Bumps" and "Upstairs and Downstairs" extend Owl's Chelm-like existence. Failing to realize the bumps at the foot of his bed are his own feet, Owl's mind runs wild with fears that the bumps will overtake him. In the end, they do, for he ends up sleeping downstairs by the fireplace, leaving the two strange bumps to "sit on my bed all by themselves."[4] Unknowingly afraid of a part of himself, it is only Owl's perception that can ever tame the strange bumps.

Unable to appreciate the simultaneous existence of his upstairs and downstairs, Owl tries in "Upstairs and Downstairs" to be in both places at once—to be two Owls at once. After exhausting himself by rushing up and down the stairs he gives up in despair and sits on the middle step.

> When I am up
> I am not down.
> When I am down
> I am not up.
> All I am is very tired.
>   (49)

Unable to enjoy each element (upstairs and downstairs) in its own manner, he ends up with nothing but frustration and a sense of loss.

Owl's actions are absurd, but they are not the failed decisions of a worldly character. It is in complete innocence that he worries that the winter is too cold and that the bumps will grow, or that the moon is a friend. This perspective is what keeps Owl at the far end of reductio ad absurdum and bound to what seems a world of nonsense. His wide-eyed, understated reactions to the absurd also make him endearing. At the same time as he represents an aspect of the reader's behavior Owl is also in need of the reader's protective eye. Frog and Toad have one another to balance their world. Owl has only the reader to keep his world from falling over the edge.

Fulfilling the role of archetypal fool, Owl also brings life to Rosenmeyer's description of the classic pastoral character as "not a thinker . . . but a perceiver of concrete sensations and beautiful things. There is humor in the limitation. . . . But, more importantly, there is strength and cheerfulness."[5] Just as Owl is a comic extension of Lobel's behavior, he is also an extension of his poetic heart. In the same interview in which he described Owl as psychotic, Lobel described *Owl at Home* as "one of the most personal books I've ever written."[6]

Both "Tear-Water Tea" and "Owl and the Moon" reflect Lobel's and Owl's poetic eye and sense of private reverie. A major chord of Lobel's pastoral world is a pantheistic honoring of objects, especially objects so familiar most fail to see them. He gives them all—flowers, wind, moon, and earth—a voice and lyric role in his stories's action.

In "Tear-Water Tea" Owl celebrates in this same pastoral tradition what others literally fail to see, the small and long-forgotten. From one perspective Owl is crying over spilt milk. A flatfooted realist would see no point in lamenting lost pencils or missing book pages. Yet from the opposite perspective Owl's litany of objects is significant. Like Stuart Little's list of important things that includes "a shaft of sunlight at the end of a dark afternoon" and "the way the back of a baby's neck smells if its mother keeps

it tidy,"[7] Owl's is an honoring of daily wonderments too easily forgotten by others. As one who is forever investing inanimate objects with life, Owl mourns objects that have lost their voice—
their life—by being abandoned.

>Songs that cannot be sung
>because the words
>have been forgotten. . . .
>
>Spoons that have fallen
>behind the stove
>and are never seen again. . . .
>
>Books that cannot
>be read
>because some of the pages
>have been torn out. . . .
>
>And pencils
>that are too short to use.
>   (32–36)

As he remembers the small and forgotten, Owl renews his vision,
sense of connection with the world, and, in turn, his joy. Smiling
brightly, Owl concludes: "'It tastes / a little bit salty, / but tear-
water tea / is always very good'" (39).

Rendering objects vivid to the imagination, Owl exists in kinship with the sublime poets,[8] yet the objects of his anthropomor-
phizing—objects of home as opposed to cosmic elements—makes
his a humorous world. The incongruity of this bonding, states
Max Sutton in "'Inverse Sublimity' in Victorian Humor," "gives
way to the pathos of the brotherly connection that is stressed by
the rustic man of feeling."[9] Owl's becomes a pastoral world where
man and objects are equals.

This "brotherly connection" is the heart of Owl's final story,
"Owl and the Moon." Alone and watching the sea, Owl befriends

the moon whom Chesterton in "A Defence of Nonsense" calls the "patroness of nonsense."[10]

> If I am looking
> at you, moon
> then you must be
> looking back at me.
> We must be
> very good friends.
>   (53)

Time and again Owl tells the moon not to follow him home as there won't be enough food or room, but once the moon does leave (behind clouds), Owl is very sad. It is only after the moon (nonsense) returns and fills his bedroom with silver light that Owl feels relaxed and truly at home again.

With nonsense as Lobel's vibrant companion throughout his life and work, *Owl at Home* is indeed one of his most personal books.

In many ways Grasshopper of *Grasshopper on the Road* is a cumulative character for Lobel. He has the joyous impulse of Toad, the maturity and orderliness of Frog, the humor and appreciation for the absurd of both mouse narrators, and the poetic eye of Owl. At the same time Grasshopper is very different. He has no home or hearth—vital ingredients of Frog and Toad stories, *Owl at Home,* and both mice anthologies. Where previous "I Can Read" characters began their stories at home, journeyed out, and returned home, Grasshopper is forever "on the road." One does not even see the home he leaves, as he is already on his journey when the story begins.

Still, as different as his story is, Grasshopper is a natural extension of Owl's (and Lobel's) experience of Arcadia as an attitude or manner of seeing rather than as a singular location. His journey is in no way a threat to his Arcadia, as it is for Ratty in *The Wind in the Willows.* Ratty is restless and wants to escape into adventure, to find what he thinks he cannot find at home. In his need for change he becomes, in Grahame's words "mechanical" and in need of a "cure." To the contented Grasshopper his journey is not a threat because his Arcadia is within him, in the manner in which he lives his life. Rather than traveling as a swashbuckler seeking adventures, Grasshopper journeys as a comic poet on an extended Victorian walk, open to the melody of experiences it will bring.

Through his serial adventures Grasshopper becomes a picaresque hero in the tradition of early film—a miniature Chaplin. There cannot be a more succinct description of Grasshopper's narrative role than Gerald Mast's of the role of the film picaro in *The Comic Mind: Comedy and the Movies:* "to bounce off the people and events around him, often, in the process, revealing the superiority of his comic bouncing to the social and human walls he hits."[11] With its gallery of character types *Grasshopper on the Road* prepares the way for *Fables,* in which the reader takes on Grasshopper's role of picaro.

The social and human walls Grasshopper "hits" are as close as Lobel comes to having a "they," as Lear did in so many of his limericks. In Lear "they" were always minor characters exerting power over the often incongruous protagonists. In *Grasshopper on the Road* "they" are the insects he encounters that insist on categorizing the world. Only the worm in "The New Home" is Grasshopper's kindred spirit. Housefly is yet another fanatical cleaner. "Rules are rules" insists mosquito, even when adhering to them is absurd. The butterflies live each day as an echo of the last and quickly answer, "No, never" when asked if they ever change anything. The beetles condemn anyone who is not exclusively a morning fan: "Anyone who loves afternoon and night can never, never be in our club."[12] And the dragonflies are so busy "zipping and zooming," they "do not have time to look at flowers" (57). All reject Grasshopper when he dares to say he has different opinions and that different opinions can coexist. Still it is grasshopper who chooses to move on. The insects may reject him, but their judgments do not affect him.

Not only do these insect characters categorize their world, but in dividing it into black or white, they lose their world. Just as one's way of seeing the world can create Arcadia, it can also destroy it. Not one of the insects has a sense of humor or an appreciation for the comic. They are embalmed with earnestness and self-importance. Grasshopper, in direct contrast, triumphs through his comic perspective. He exhibits Wylie Sypher's view of comedy, which leads to an internal pastoral world:

> Comedy can be a means of mastering our disillusions when we are caught in a dishonest or stupid society. After we recognize the misdoings, the blunders, we can liberate ourselves by a confident wise laughter that brings a catharsis of our discontent. We see the flaws in things, but we do not always need to concede the victory, even if we live in a human world. If we can laugh wisely enough at ourselves and others, the sense of guilt, dismay, anxiety, or fear can be lifted. Unflinching and undaunted we see *where we are*.[13]

By neither denying nor accepting the insects' judgments, Grasshopper lives above their categories and is more at home on the road than the insects are in their homes. For Grasshopper, the journey is as Arcadian as wooded cottages are for Frog and Toad and Owl.

> Grasshopper was tired.
> He lay down in a soft place.
> He knew that in the morning
> the road would be there,
> taking him on and on
> to wherever
> he wanted to go.
>
>   (62)

The one story in *Grasshopper on the Road* that doesn't illustrate the antipastoralist rigidity of "they" is "A New House," which instead echoes Grasshopper's own perspective. Only intending to have lunch, Grasshopper discovers the apple he is eating is also Worm's house. Grasshopper apologizes, but the apple

starts rolling down the hill picking up speed as it goes, a visualization of reductio ad absurdum. Worm's cries of alarm make a
comic list of incongruities: "My bathtub / is in the living room. /
My bed is in the kitchen! / . . . My floor is on the ceiling! / My attic
is in the cellar" (20–21). The apple house doesn't stop until it hits
a tree at the bottom of the hill and is smashed to pieces. Another
worm might have been even angrier, but Worm, like Grasshopper,
knows that home (Arcadia) is more than four walls or the inside
of a particular apple. Worm is open to change and possibility. He
simply climbs up the same apple tree that destroyed his old home
and says, "This is a fine time for me to find a new house" (23).
Seeing that the tree is filled with apples, Grasshopper smiles and
goes on his way. He knows as does Worm that only his external
home has been destroyed, and that, if anything, Worm's real
home, his inner home, will be enriched by the change.

Uncle Elephant is significant within Lobel's work from several
perspectives. In the seven years from its publication to his death
Lobel wrote no other "I Can Read" texts and only one other plotted story, the folklike *Ming Lo Moves the Mountain* (1982). (*A
Rose in My Garden* illustrated by Anita Lobel is more poem than
story and *The Turnaround Wind* is not so much a story as a visual
experience.) In *Uncle Elephant* Lobel wrote his longest single narrative and one different in form from the rest of his "I Can Read"
texts. Rather than the vignettes of Frog and Toad stories and *Owl
at Home* that can be read in any order, or the anthologies of separate tales in *Mouse Tales* and *Mouse Soup, Uncle Elephant* is in
chapters, each building on the last.

While Lobel in a 1977 interview described *Owl at Home* as his
most personal work, *Uncle Elephant,* published four years later,
is certainly his most autobiographical. Told from the abandoned
child's point of view, it is Lobel's only first-person narrative and
the only book published after *The Bears of the Air* (1965) to feature a child character. With his father in California, his mother
off at her daily job, Lobel, like his young elephant narrator, was
raised by much older adults, his grandmother who was "strong
and well organized . . . [with] enough energy to deal with a cir-

cumstance that surely could not have seemed ideal to her"[14] and his even older grandfather who tended the family garden.

Uncle Elephant is Lobel's only adult character, except for grumpy Grandfather Bear in *The Bears of the Air,* who functions in a parental role. He is also more than any other character the one who sees the world through Lobel's creative eye. Upon finding his nephew, Uncle Elephant says, "Now come out of this dark place"[15] and introduces him to the pastoral world (gardens, song, and humor) and the perspective that creates it. It is exactly what Lobel is saying to his readers with each book: "Now come out of this dark place and into my pastoral world."

Uncle Elephant and Lobel are the antithesis of Kenneth Grahame's weary, embittered, and destructive adults or Olympians who can no longer see Arcadia. Whereas Grahame laments, "I certainly did once inhabit Arcady. Can it be I too have become an Olympian?"[16] Lobel and Uncle Elephant remain Arcadians and lead the child into the pastoral world. Uncle Elephant could be described, as was Lobel in *Newsweek,* as one of the lucky few who has retained the ability "to see the world with child-like wonder"[17]—a blithe spirit.

While Lobel invites readers into the pastoral world with his stories and poems, Uncle Elephant literally trumpets with the dawn and formally introduces his nephew to Arcadia, a land in this case found away from his original home.

> "I have planted
> all these flowers myself.
> Come outside
> and let me introduce you
> to everyone,"
> said Uncle Elephant.
> "Roses, daisies,
> daffodils and marigolds,
> I want you
> to meet my nephew."
> I bowed to the flowers.

> Uncle Elephant
> was pleased.
> "This garden
> is my favorite place
> in the world,"
> said Uncle Elephant.
> "It is my own kingdom."
> "If this is your kingdom,"
> I said,
> "are you the king?"
> "I suppose I am,"
> said Uncle Elephant.
> "If you are the king,"
> I said,
> "I must be the prince."
> "Of course,"
> said Uncle Elephant,
> "you *must* be the prince.!"
> We made ourselves
> crowns of flowers.
>   (28–30)

It is a crowning passage in Lobel's prose and rings with such truth because Uncle Elephant lives his daily life as a pastoral poet. For him music, story, and laughter are natural expressions and paths away from pain and sorrow. When aching from the "creaks," Uncle Elephant tells his nephew:

> "If you let me
> tell you a story,
> I am sure all of my creaks
> will go away."
>   (36)

Whereas Frog and Toad tell one another stories to make the other feel better, Uncle Elephant understands the artist's personal benefits in creating a story for others. His story is naturally about

From *Uncle Elephant* by Arnold Lobel. © 1981 by Arnold Lobel. Reprinted by permission of Harper & Row, p. 29. Original dimensions 9.5 cm × 11 cm.

his nephew and himself. In it, when threatened by a fierce lion, they literally trumpet out his teeth with song. And, when they are lost, it is little elephant's sharp eyes from atop his uncle's shoulders that find their path home and to the end of the story.

Later when a family photograph makes both uncle and nephew sad, nonsense (reductio ad absurdum) is the antidote. Uncle Elephant puts on all the clothes he owns at once.

> Uncle Elephant
> was a pile of clothes
> with two big ears.

First I smiled.
Then I giggled.
Then I laughed.
We both laughed so hard
we forgot to feel sad.

(50)

Love of nonsense and its restorative powers are not the only themes that echo from earlier Lobel stories. Uncle Elephant and little elephant, like the wishing mouse in *Mouse Tales,* discover that there is as much pleasure in granting the wish of another as in getting one's own wish. When they discover that the "magic lamp" they are rubbing is also the home of a spider, they are able to grant his wish for peace and quiet by leaving his house alone.

Though not chronological equals, as Frog and Toad appear to be, Uncle Elephant and little elephant are loving companions and kindred spirits. Few illustrations of humans in picture books evoke love's bond as thoroughly as do Lobel's illustrations of the two pachyderms with their trunks gently intertwined. Their dialogue and actions are equally warm and caring. Like Very Tall Mouse and Very Short Mouse of *Mouse Tales* who share the rainbow, their friendship and pastoral perspective give them a world of beauty to share despite their physical differences.

Overt death does not exist (nor could it) within Lobel's pastoral, but in *Uncle Elephant* it is clearly at the edges. The story opens with little elephant's parents being lost in a sailing disaster. Their survival, which brings the book to a joyful conclusion, also marks the end, the death, of the tangible Arcadia little elephant shared with Uncle Elephant. And while never discussed, the eventuality of death is inherent in "creaky" Uncle Elephant who is long past the chronological noon of his life. Their farewell on the book's last page carries with it a sense of finality and resistance to it, yet is softened by honoring memories.

"[These] were wonderful days,"
[said Uncle Elephant.]
"They all passed too fast."

We promised
to see each other often.
Uncle Elephant
kissed me
good night
and closed
the door.

(64)

It is a moment of sadness and transition, but the gift remains. Little elephant has learned by example that Arcadia need not fade because one grows older on the calendar. He, too, can create his own kingdom of flowers, song, story, and companionship.

A concluding look at *Uncle Elephant* in relation to *The Bears of the Air* illumines not only one of Lobel's primary themes (one creates one's own Arcadia) but his growth as a writer expressing that theme. In *The Bears of the Air* Lobel clearly knew what he valued, but still felt he had to argue to prove his beliefs. Grandfather Bear spends all his time lecturing on the things bears should do to be good bears, and the young bears battle back with the things they have fun doing instead. Though he wrote in support of the cubs, Lobel's tone was as much one of lecturing as was Grandfather Bear's. The cubs win the debate, but the story's focus remains on the confrontation between generations and activities rather than on the pastoral perspective itself. Lobel told, but failed to evoke.

In contrast, neither Uncle Elephant nor little elephant argue or lecture, and neither does Lobel's text. Both Lobel and Uncle Elephant subtly create an atmosphere that is so alive that both little elephant and the reader enter it easily. As a writer, Lobel evolved from the uncertain child trying to convince the authorities of this theme to the seasoned and self-assured adult who is so certain of his perspective he has no need to debate to defend it. Uncle Elephant doesn't need to talk about the value of song, play, or nonsense. He lives it. He draws from his own life, as Lobel came to do in his best works, to create songs and stories that *create* for little elephant the pastoral world he treasures. The arguments of the bears in *The Bears of the Air* over the value of song was replaced by the song itself in *Uncle Elephant* and the accompanying joie de vivre.

After *Uncle Elephant* Lobel's primary work moved from narratives with pastoral settings to the primary pastoral pastime, song. With *Pigericks, Whiskers & Rhymes,* and *Mother Goose* Lobel celebrated nonsense and song, and with *A Rose in My Garden* wrote a song of the garden itself.

Both Uncle Elephant and Lobel are examples of the pastoral view summed up in the proverb: "who sings, charms his ills."[18] Just as Uncle Elephant created a story for little elephant to forget his own creaks and wrote a song to affirm their relationship, Lobel wrote *Uncle Elephant* as a joyful celebration to dissipate his sadness and bitterness over his grandmother's enfeeblement: "In an effort to exorcise my feelings, I have written a book . . . about the elderly person that I would wish my grandmother to be."[19]

Though the singing of any song can offer a temporary escape or healing, Uncle Elephant and Lobel do much more. They know the content of their songs and stories must come from within themselves if they are to be both truthful and of any value to themselves and others. Understanding this, their act of creating becomes Arcadia.

9

A Garden of Tales and Bawdy Verse

I don't think I could exist without the past.[1]

While Lobel only illustrated two folktales and two volumes of Mother Goose, thirteen of his texts, including *Fables,* are related to folklore. If one includes his fablelike "I Can Read" stories, the number swells to twenty-four. The fable, which was in form to Lobel as the song was to Schubert, has already been explored, leaving this chapter to focus on his longer folk literature and Mother Goose, both of which dominate his later work.

The pastoral world the folktale ensures and its innate element of nonsense made it a natural facet of Lobel's work. In keeping with his voice and perspective, Lobel approached tales not as an actor looking for star-making vehicles, but in the traditional manner as described by folklorist Carl-Herman Tillhagen. The storyteller, states Tillhagen, is a gardener "who selects from the main wildflowers those he specially loves, cares for them and cultivates them and thus grows more beautiful and durable species."[2] The folk elements Lobel selected to preserve were (in style and material)[3] in keeping with the body of his work: nonsense, humor, and the archetypal extension of behavior to its essence through extremes (reductio ad absurdum).

Lobel's 1971 edition of *Hansel and Gretel* begins and ends as does so much of his work with warm images of home. Leaving primary focus on the text, he created more of an illuminated manuscript than a picture book. Except for the one doublespread of Hansel and Gretel finding the witch's hut, all the illustrations are framed, smaller than page size, and interspersed with the text. Images of Hansel and Gretel are often as surrounded by text as they are by the forbidding woods and the eye of the witch. Faces, rather than panoramas, are the heart of his illustrations, and the heart or emotions are the center of each image. By "reading" the illustrations alone, one can follow the characters' emotional arcs through the story. The father's confusion and conflicting loyalties are particularly well done, exemplifying how Lobel establishes the characters through their reactions to events. Dominated by shadow and forms built up by pencil cross-hatching, the entire book evokes the hushed uncertainty of forests and nights, making the final light-filled images especially joyful. Well received when first published, it was reissued in 1985. The *Horn Book* found it a "quiet completely effective interpretation"[4] and storyteller/folklorist Anne Pellowski stated in her *New York Times Book Review* that Lobel was one of only a few who "comes close to the spirit of intimacy and homeliness in the Grimm stories."[5]

Published between *Frog and Toad Are Friends* and *Frog and Toad Together*, Lobel's work on *Hansel and Gretel* shows his growing awareness of story as human behavior (emotion) creating and reacting to event rather than being event alone. This awareness enabled him to invest *Hansel and Gretel* with an emotional depth that was missing in his own early folk-style books, *Prince Bertram the Bad, Giant John,* and *The Great Blueness*. Magic and the magical were placed in secondary position and the fascinating everyday lives of people came front and center.

The nearly ten years that separate *The Great Blueness* and *How the Rooster Saved the Day* (1977) were far from being void of folklore. Lobel's own writing had been growing with each book of fablelike "I Can Read" stories, and his illustrative assignments for texts by others included Jameson's retelling of *The Clay Pot Boy* and Duran's folk-style *Hildilid's Night*. Working on his cinematic illustrations for the latter two clearly improved his ear for folk rhythms. Several earlier illustrators whose work he admired and often viewed, including Caldecott, Crane, and Potter, had also worked with folklore.

Anita Lobel's work, which was evolving only a few feet from his, was filled with folklore and could not have helped but be influential. Raised in Europe, Anita was completely at home with folklore in both text and image. "I must have been influenced by old fairy tales," she told *Publishers Weekly* in 1971. "Tales that have a logical beginning, a middle and then retribution in the end for someone and happiness for someone else."[6] Bookjackets and reviews of her early books often referred to her decorative peasant art. In the years between *Giant John* and *How the Rooster Saved the Day* Anita Lobel had illustrated *The Wisest Man in the World* (1968) and *How the Tsar Drinks His Tea* (1971) both told by Benjamin Elkin, *Three Rolls and a Doughnut* (1970) told by Mirra Ginsburg, and *Clever Kate* (1973) told by Elizabeth Shub. Her own texts during the same period included the folk-flavored *Sven's Bridge* (1965), *The Troll Music* (1966), *A Birthday for the Princess* (1973), and *King Rooster, Queen Hen* (1975). In other words, folklore was a regular part of Lobel's ongoing world.

The field of children's literature has had many couples who both illustrated, but Arnold and Anita Lobel were unique. While the Petershams, the d'Aulaires, the Provensens, the Dillons, and Aruego and Dewey (both during and after marriage) work or worked as a team to create single images, the Lobels (like John Burningham and Helen Oxenbury of England) worked independently. When they did finally collaborate on four books, all were sparked by Anita's artwork and Arnold, as writer, made no contribution to the illustrations.

Inspired by Anita's work on a large stained-glass rooster and her own book *King Rooster, Queen Hen,* Lobel wrote *How the Rooster Saved the Day,* then realized it was really a story for Anita to do. The next three texts, *A Treeful of Pigs, On Market Street,* and *The Rose in My Garden* were written specifically for Anita, much as a writer/director writes roles with a certain actor in mind.

With *How The Rooster Saved the Day* and *A Treeful of Pigs*

Lobel employed not only character types from folklore, as he had done in early texts, but also their logic and rhythm. Both titles share Western folklore's primary pattern of repetition and pivot on standard motifs of feigning deafness to outsmart a villain and of outsmarting laziness with wit. Blending these basic folk elements and his fascination with human behavior, Lobel became as fully involved in his stories as he had with his childhood tales of Hollywood playmates. Believing in them, he found his voice growing sure and trusting with none of the tentativeness that had weakened *Giant John*.

What makes both texts identifiably Lobel's is their integral sense of nonsense. Rooster convinces the thief he is a fool by telling him that he has been quacking, barking, oinking, and mooing. The child reader, like the thief, readily sees the nonsense, laughs with the thief, yet soon finds that the nonsense had not really been so foolish after all. In his eagerness to prove the Rooster a nonsense-talking fool, the thief proceeds to show him how to crow up the sun and, by accident, literally does so himself. Afraid of being recognized, the thief flees and the rooster has saved the day by the logic of nonsense and the nonsense of those (like the thief) who adhere too closely to logic.

The cleverness that triumphs in *A Treeful of Pigs* is also based on nonsense. After begging for pigs to raise, the farmer is too lazy to get out of bed and do the needed chores. Each time he is challenged by his wife the farmer makes another nonsensical promise of when he'll work, for example, when pigs rain from the sky. By bringing her lazy husband's nonsense to life each time he promises, the woman eventually turns the tables and tosses his own ploy back at him. The inversion of the story's pattern causes change both in rhythms and content, and the story soon ends with a celebratory supper served up by the newly reformed husband.

Lobel's text for *On Market Street* was inspired by Anita Lobel's 1977 poster for the Children's Book Council. Featuring a bookseller made out of books, the poster had been inspired by seventh-century French trade engravings. Primarily an alphabet book of purchases set in the nebulous world of Mother Goose, *On Market Street* closes with a touch of pure Lobel.

> But I was glad on Market Street,
> These coins I brought to spend,
> I spent them all on Market Street . . .
> on presents for a friend.[7]

That friend, in keeping with his work of the period, was naturally a cat. Anita included two more friends as puppets on the toy merchant's hands, Lobel's own Frog and Toad. *On Market Street* was selected as a Caldecott Honor Book, Anita Lobel's first such award.

In the March 1984 issue of the *Junior Literary Guild Catalog* Lobel explained how he and Anita had both looked for years for a way to make Anita's talent with flowers the centerpiece for a book. Knowing few children are intrigued with flowers had kept the project at bay. Then, while "rereading and enjoying" "The House That Jack Built," Lobel realized "that just as the images in that rhyme grow and proliferate—so do the flowers in the garden" and wondered if that cumulative rhyme structure could "possibly be turned into the garden that Anita grew."[8] As folklore's best-known reductio ad absurdum plot line, it was certainly well suited to Lobel's writing. Still, never satisfied with creating mere echoes, he added a circular touch to *A Rose in My Garden* by having the final character, "the cat with the tattered ear," chase "the field mouse shaking with fear" through the garden, thus bringing about his own punishment by waking up the "bee that sleeps on the rose in my garden" and getting stung on the nose. The book's reception was as warm and welcoming as the receptions of the three other joint titles had been, and it was selected as a Boston Globe-Horn Book Honor Book for illustration. Roger Swain's description of *A Rose in My Garden* in the *New York Times Book Review* not only captured the atmosphere of that particular book, but also of Lobel's entire fictional world. It is "a book one can settle back down into with the same anticipation of comfort and pleasure as settling down into a well-stuffed armchair with flowered upholstery."[9]

Ming Lo Moves the Mountain (1981) may be seen as significant to Lobel's work in many ways. It is his only text with an Asian setting, the only folk-style text he illustrated of his own writing after *The Great Blueness,* and by fate, his last plotted narrative. It is also pure Lobel, yet as Natalie Babbitt wrote in *Book World,* to say it is Lobel is misleading because "one of the things that is admirable about Lobel's work is that he is able always to adapt his style to the demands of the story, and that is a rare quality. It demonstrates courage, flexibility, and responsiveness, three of the factors which contribute to his solid and well-deserved reputation."[10] In other words, he had reached in his writing the very quality he valued in illustrating: "a repertory of styles at his command—like an actor switching from role to role."[11]

What makes *Ming Lo Moves the Mountain* true Lobel and perhaps explains why he elected to illustrate it, rather than have Anita do so, is the quiet gentleness of its foolishness and its truth that in the end happiness is often a matter of one's perspective. And, if one is happy, perhaps apparent foolishness is neither bad nor absurd after all.

Quite naturally for Lobel, *Ming Lo* begins and ends at home. The twist is that between the beginning and the end the house, as well as the characters, go on a journey to the pastoral. Ming Lo and his wife live in a classical Chinese landscape painting, yet are so close to the moutain everyone admires, they are forced to live in its shade, tolerate damage from falling rocks, and endure the frequent rains from the clouds that create the mountain's mystical aura. As self-centered as a child, Ming Lo and his equally Chelm-like (Owl-like) wife decide to move not themselves, but the mountain. It is here that the cycle of action begins. Much like the rabbi in the tale "It Could Always Be Worse," Lobel's wise man seems as foolish as the fool until his actions suddenly, in the end, prove to be wise in their cumulative effect. When pushing with a tree, making noise, and offering bread all fail to move the mountain, the wise man tells Ming Lo and his wife to dismantle their house, close their eyes, and do the dance of the moving mountain. Much to their delight the dance (which is nothing more than walking backwards) works; they rebuild their home and live out their days in pastoral happiness and weather, believing they had made the mountain move. For Ming Lo absurdity brings Arcadia.

Visually *Ming Lo Moves the Mountain* is as softly hued as the mist around the mountain and has the translucent sheen of porcelain. All lines and shapes are as circular as the story itself. The use of ink markers creates individual lines that are themselves wider, rounder, and softer in appearance than pencil or pen. Rather than trying to mimic Chinese painting, Lobel used his emotional response to Chinese art as the base for evoking the same through his own style. It was done, like his work with folk elements, with the care of a gardener sharing what he most enjoyed.

Told with ingenuous sincerity, the humor of *Ming Lo Moves the Mountain* is that of the wise man himself (and Lobel, too)—a gentle, knowing smile without judgment. Quiet in setting, characters, and execution, *Ming Lo Moves the Mountain* is closer in both spirit and evocation to the pastoral Frog and Toad volumes than to the brisk pace and broad comic action of *How the Rooster Saved the Day* and *A Treeful of Pigs*. Just as illustrating the words of others gave Lobel a chance to stretch and make images very different from those matching his own stories, writing for another illustrator he knew so well also gave him a chance to stretch and write in a voice that was slightly different from that of his pastoral "I Can Read" stories and the tongue-in-cheek elegance of *Fables*.

Because of his longtime interest in nonsense, verse, and Edward Lear, it was only natural for Lobel to turn to the "grandmother of nonsense,"[12] Mother Goose, as his interest in singing increased. The rhymes of Mother Goose have been the pastoral songs of children for centuries. Mother Goose is filled with the anthropomorphism and animated objects that fill Lobel's work, but his first book of Mother Goose rhymes, *Gregory Griggs,* was, at least on the surface, a new departure. Lobel was forever trying to do books that were different from those he had done before. As discussed in chapter 4, he chose to feature only lesser-known rhymes and only those with human characters.

Rather than a departure from his work, the rhymes Lobel selected—once again with the care of a gardener—were actually a sure step toward the heart of his work—absurd human behavior and amiable coexistence. All the characters are cousins to the humans in Edward Lear's limericks, which Lobel had long enjoyed, and are direct forefathers of the rhymes Lobel would later create for his masterful *Whiskers & Rhymes*. One rhyme selected for *Gregory Griggs* (and later his *Mother Goose*) is particularly interesting in light of Lear's long poems and Lobel's *The Man Who Took the Indoors Out*.

> Alas! alas! for Miss Mackay!
> Her knives and forks have run away;
> And when the cups and spoons are going,
> She's sure there is no way of knowing.
>
> (*GG*, 44)

When Lobel journeyed out to Mother Goose, it was truly a circular journey home.

By the time he began work on *The Random House Book of Mother Goose* in January 1983, he was well acquainted with the classic rhymes. *Gregory Griggs, A Rose in My Garden,* and the Mother Goose-inspired *Whiskers & Rhymes* had filled much of the last few years, and his genuine enjoyment of the rhymes made the project an energetic match: "If they felt flat to me when I read them, I didn't use them. And some of them I loved."[13] They were not in his eyes delicate antiques that had once had life, but instead "bawdy and naughty" nonsense songs that were very much alive and that formed a "lusty body of literature."[14] "Most of the poems came from the 18th century, when people used to wipe their mouths with their hair," he told *Publishers Weekly*. "I hope my book expresses that."[15]

Whether or not he completely captured the earthy manners of the period, Lobel's characters, both humans and animals (here they are completely interchangeable unless specified in the text), fill the pages with the zest and fullness of a week-long pre-Lenten feast. Pages are designed in a constantly changing manner so that the only rhythm in the book is that of continual movement and change. By turn, some pages are a gathering of separate images, a large tableau depicting several rhymes at once, or a single verse, some stretching to fill a massive doublespread. Everyone is glimpsed in mid-action and emotions are intense. Hannah Ban-try in the pantry is thoroughly gluttonous and is no longer even trying to hide as in *Gregory Griggs*. A vital element in Lobel's approach to Mother Goose was his recognition of the pain behind the humor:

> Mother Goose is not a funny business. Most of them are great comedic pieces, and as we know, comedy is not created out of pleasant things. It is created out of pain, and Mother Goose is a master of using pain as an inspiration for her comedy. And we know from Aesop to Charlie Chaplin, right on through Woody Allen, we know that what is painful is also funny and Mother Goose is full of that. Most of the people in Mother Goose aren't terribly happy.[16]

This awareness gave all his images a greater resonance, for he approached the characters as individuals with a story rather than as toys.

At times Lobel tackled the violence in some verses, which he saw as violent in the way children love to be scared. "Goosey, goosey, gander" and "Wee Willie Winkie" are truly menacing in tone, being softened only by Lobel's stylistic distance from realism. For other rhymes he offered new interpretations that altered the violence of their action. The three blind mice, for example, are not really blind at all in his illustration, but faking beggars able to flee at the first sign of the carving knife.

As in *Whiskers & Rhymes,* Lobel's colors are rich and palpable, and he builds his line of varying media and rhythm to near-sculptural shapes. The trace of both his pencil and brush invest the entire book with a playful spontaneity. No matter how often one opens the book, the images have the freshness and immediacy of having just been completed.

The match of Lobel and Mother Goose was clearly one of kindred spirits. Lobel's personal goal of using every ounce of his experience[17] produced one of the most lively collections in years. Filled to the brim with his sense of theater, the absurd, song, and nonsense as pastoral holiday, Lobel's *Mother Goose* is a garden of rhymes that is certain to last.

10

Ha Ha He!

Books are something where a child can find a gentleness that he can't find anywhere else.[1]

It is at once paradoxical and fitting that Lobel's pastoral voice
came to maturity and that his stories met with wide acclaim during the late sixties and the seventies. Socially, the United States
was experiencing great unrest and division. Literature for children had fixed its eye on issue-bound realism and was, as often
as not, as noisy as the voices in the streets and Senate chambers.
With the intention of creating social awareness, equality, and
change, much of children's literature had, as writer June Jordan
eloquently stated in 1973 drained realism of half its truth—its
love and hope. Jordan called for books that did not "simply exac-
erbate the howling of our angry, fearful, starved-out spirits."[2] It
was a time desperately in need of gentleness, hope, and good
news.

When Frog first ran up the path to Toad's house in 1970 to
wake him up into spring, children's literature began to wake up,
too (albeit just as slowly), into the beginning of a warmer era.
Without issues or banners, Lobel quietly accomplished through
his anthropomorphic characters and fablelike tales what the social realists had so often failed to do. He created a literature that

exemplified within its stories equality, included everyone, and treated the reader as an equal.

Rather than debating the lack of or the right to a good life, Lobel literally created the experience of a good life for his readers—a life of unity created through the sharing of story, song, and laughter at shared absurdities. "The great use of the idyllic in literature," states C. S. Lewis, "is to find and illustrate the good—to give a real value to the 'x' about which political algebra can then work." Lobel, as Lewis believed of William Morris, brought "back a sentiment that a man could really live by."[3]

In his film version of *Frog and Toad Together* director John Matthews extends Toad's scenes of reading to his frightened seeds in "The Garden." Toad's selection of poetry (via Matthews) is an excerpt from William Blake's "Laughing Song." There could not be a more appropriate poem for encouraging fearful seeds nor one more representative of Lobel's writing spirit.

> When the air does laugh with our merry wit,
> And the green hill laughs with the noise of it; . . .
> Come live & be merry, and join with me,
> To sing the sweet chorus of "Ha, Ha, He!"[4]

While other voices of his time were announcing "You should," "We deserve," "If only we could," and "Look what you've done" and focusing on the walls between people, Lobel instinctively sang "come join with me and sing the sweet chorus." That sweet chorus was his pastoral humor based in celebrating our shared hearts and absurdities. In doing so, he revealed more similarities than differences between people on either side of the walls, dismantled those walls from within, and found a garden.

The garden has always been a place not so much seen as experienced totally, and Lobel's invitation to the Arcadian meadow is actually an invitation to become a pastoral poet like Uncle Elephant. It is an invitation to experience the creating of one's own garden through humor and the act of creation. Interested in sharing rather than dividing, and revealing rather than lecturing, Lobel always leaves room for the reader to enter his work and, in

effect, create the story with him. This attitude turns his stories—
both those set in the pastoral garden like the *Frog and Toad* series and those evoking the same garden through the holiday of
nonsense such as *Mouse Tales*—into a type of poetic garden themselves, which can be experienced as a "series of steps, each a focus
of meditation, in which the expression of the artist mingles with
the interpretation of the viewer."[5]

While this metaphor is true of Lobel's work in general, it is
particularly appropriate when his primary works are experienced
in the order in which they were created, each extending the previous experience. One enters the garden through the pastoral
friendship of Frog and Toad, their comic behavior, and their love
of home; shares Owl's innocence and poetic eye, which invests life
in everything; encounters Grasshopper on the road, who understands that the truest garden, the truest home, is not so much a
place seen but an experience and perspective one creates within
wherever one goes; and finally meets Uncle Elephant, a pastoral
poet, who confirms by example that one can create—as did
Lobel—one's own Arcadia through the sharing of nonsense, song,
and story. Scattered throughout this garden like bright red pop-
pies are the nonsense, songs, and stories themselves—*Mouse
Tales, Mouse Soup, Pigericks, Whiskers & Rhymes,* and *The Man
Who Took the Indoors Out*—each a pastoral interlude of its own.
Once experienced, this pastoral perspective lives on within the
reader (and the field of children's literature) and nourishes his
daily life, just as it does for little elephant and the poets who
acquired "certain habits of looking and thinking *inside* the garden . . . [and] found them equally serviceable *beyond* the ha-ha
[garden wall or moat]."[6]

What makes Lobel's garden of stories unique and hardy, hence
more resonant and lasting, is his approach, his ability to enrich
the familiar, his craftsmanship, and humor. Forever interested in
home and daily life, Lobel wrote with the heart of an intimist and
the eye of a minimalist. Size or length of story was not as important as the depth and truth of the experience. He knew, like Alexander Pope, that three inches of a garden (or story) could be as
fulfilling and involving as threescore acres,[7] and that, at times, a

single blossom is more aesthetically pleasing and warming than a bouquet. Just as Owl finds poetry in a forgotten stubby pencil, Lobel finds the poetry in Owl's finding the pencil poetic, and in other supposedly mundane domestic scenes such as overeating, cleaning house, sharing tales, and secretly raking another's leaves.

His minimalist's eye enabled Lobel to extend the early-reader book to a level from which it seemingly has no place to go. Turning every apparent limitation—brevity of structure, language, and scope—into an asset by writing pastoral vignettes of home and hearth, Lobel, more than any other, established the early reader as a genuine literary genre.

Lobel also found the fable's natural distillation a complementary form for his pastoral vignettes and extended the fable within its boundaries as well. By writing serial fables based on continuing characters, he was able, through dialogue, to create breathing, rounded characters rather than the standard symbolic masks. When he confined himself to single fables and one-story characters, he was still able to broaden characterization through his use of moral, which refracts off the story and sparks the reader's own extension of character and situation.

Two of the four primary elements in Lobel's work—friendship, home, laughter, and story—are nursed by legions of sentimental and insipid writers. Lobel, however, did not simply wax nostalgic. Like Uncle Elephant, he transformed the "clash and clank" of daily life into story and song. "When I can put myself into a frame of mind to be able to share with the reader my problems and my own sense of life's travail, then I discover that I am working in top form."[8] Lobel's innate sense of humor and craftsmanship prevented his sharing of travail from becoming the romanticized bleeding of a self-conscious poet. Stories of laughter, not anger, had brought him from the outside in. As a craftsman, a journeyman writer, he fashioned "the raw material of experience, his own and that of others, in a solid, useful, and unique way."[9] His "top form" was a celebration of his inner life—the joy of seeing himself and the world through Blake's sweet chorus of "Ha Ha He!"

Like nonsense, the garden or pastoral experience must alternate with its opposite in order to maintain its full richness and value. The garden is always most refreshing when experienced anew. Not bound to any time or style, Lobel's pastoral stories and rhymes wait on shelves, like his own collection of beloved books, till the reader needs a respite from the "vicissitudes of life."

Though Arcadia can never be reached by a map and Arnold Lobel is gone, both will always be as near as sitting back in a stuffed armchair—like Mouse in *Mouse Soup* after his escape from hungry Weasel—and reading again his fables, songs, and "I Can Reads," for that is where he still resides and forever shares the renewing song of the shepherd's reed flute.

From *Mouse Soup* by Arnold Lobel. © 1977 by Arnold Lobel. Reprinted by permission of Harper & Row, p. 64. Original dimensions 7 cm × 5.5 cm.

Notes and References

Preface

1. Quoted in Roni Natov and Geraldine DeLuca, "An Interview with Arnold Lobel," *Lion and the Unicorn* 1 (1977):73.
2. Margery Fisher, *Who's Who in Children's Books: A Treasury of the Familiar Characters of Childhood* (New York: Holt, 1975), 113.
3. Jacqueline Gmuca, "Arnold Lobel," in *Twentieth-Century Children's Writers* (New York: St. Martins, 1983), 493.
4. Thomas G. Rosenmeyer, *The Green Cabinet: Theocritus and the European Pastoral Lyric* (Berkeley: University of California Press, 1969), 32.

Chapter One

1. James Marshall, "Arnold Lobel," *Horn Book* 64 (May/June 1988):328.
2. "Frog and Toad: a Short History," *Claremont Reading Conference Yearbook* 42 (1978):148.
3. Ibid.
4. Ibid.
5. Eudora Welty, "The House of Willa Cather," in *The Eye of the Story: Selected Essays and Reviews* (New York: Random, 1977), 48.
6. Henri Matisse, "Notes of a Painter, 1908," in *Matisse on Art,* ed. Jack D. Flam (London: Phaidon, 1973), 38.
7. Rosenmeyer, *Green Cabinet,* 198.
8. Gaston Bachelard, *The Poetics of Space,* trans. Maria Jolas (Boston: Beacon Press, 1969), xxxi.
9. Quoted in Natov and DeLuca, "Interview," 94.
10. Ibid., 85.
11. Blue Calhoun, *The Pastoral Vision of William Morris: The Earthly Paradise* (Athens: University of Georgia Press, 1975), 76.
12. Faye Leeper, "Talking and Touching: A Function of Storytelling," in *Paisanos: A Folklore Miscellany,* ed. Francis Edward Abernethy (Austin, Tex.: Encino Press, 1978), 145.

13. "A Good Picture Book Should . . . ," in *Celebrating Children's Books: Essays on Children's Literature in Honor of Zena Sutherland,* ed. Betsy Hearne and Marilyn Kaye (New York: Lothrop, 1981), 75.

14. Hilda van Stockum, "Caldecott's Pictures in Motion," in *The Illustrator's Notebook,* ed. Lee Kingman (Boston: Horn Book, 1978), 38.

15. "A Good Picture Book," *Celebrating,* 79–80.

16. Lao Tzu quoted by Uri Shulevitz, *Rain Rain Rivers* (New York: Farrar, 1969).

17. Theocritus, translated and quoted by Rosenmeyer, *Green Cabinet,* 105.

18. Quoted in Lucy Rollin, "The Astonished Witness Disclosed: An Interview with Arnold Lobel," *Children's Literature in Education* 15 (Winter 1984):192.

19. Rosenmeyer, *Green Cabinet,* 105.

20. "A Rabbit Song," Kerlan Collection.

21. Quoted in *Books Are by People,* ed. Lee Bennett Hopkins (New York: Citation Press, 1969), 159.

22. Quoted in Pamela Lewis, "Fables of Their Own Making," *Houston Post,* 12 April 1981, 3BB.

23. William Empson, *Some Versions of Pastoral* (1950; reprint, New York: New Directions, 1974), 3–23.

24. "A Good Picture Book," *Celebrating,* 75.

25. Quoted in Susan Hood, "A Crocodile's Terror and an Elephant's Error—That's What Arnold Lobel's *Fables* Are Made of!" *Instructor* 90 (May 1981):35.

26. Christopher Fry, "Comedy," in *Comedy: Meaning and Form,* ed. Robert W. Corrigan (San Francisco: Chandler, 1965), 15.

27. Quoted in "Arnold Lobel . . . the Natural Illustrator . . . the Entertainer," *Early Years* 11 (November 1980):34.

28. Quoted in Natov and DeLuca, "Interview," 83–84.

29. Quoted in David W. McCullough, "Arnold Lobel and Friends," *New York Times Book Review,* 11 November 1979, 69.

30. "Birthdays and Beginnings," *Theory into Practice* 21 (Autumn 1982):323.

31. Quoted in McCullough, "Friends," 54.

32. Ibid.

33. E. B. White, *Stuart Little* (New York: Harper & Row, 1945), 98.

34. Peter V. Marinelli, *Pastoral* (London: Methuen, 1971), 49.

35. "Frog," *Claremont,* 151.

36. Quoted in Natov and DeLuca, "Interview," 86.

37. "Frog," *Claremont,* 152.

38. "Birthdays," *Theory,* 322.

39. Quoted in *Something About the Author,* vol. 6 (Detroit: Gale Research, 1974), 148.

40. Paul Binding, *Lorca: The Gay Imagination* (London: GMP, 1985), 100.

41. Edward L. Ruhe, "Pastoral Paradigms and Displacements, with Some Proposals," in *Survivals of Pastoral,* ed. Richard F. Hardin (Lawrence: University of Kansas Publications, 1979), 114.

42. Fred Miller Robinson, "Nonsense and Sadness in Donald Barthelme and Edward Lear," *South Atlantic Quarterly* 80 (Spring 1981):176.

43. Quoted in Faith McNulty, "Children's Books for Christmas," *New Yorker,* 1 December 1980, 212.

44. Quoted in Nancy S. Hands, *Illustrating Children's Books: A Guide to Drawings, Printing, and Publishing* (New York: Prentice-Hall, 1986), 99.

45. Quoted in *Something About the Author,* vol. 51 (Detroit: Gale Research, 1988), 115.

46. Quoted in *Arnold Lobel: Autobiographical Brochure* (New York: Harper & Row, 1985).

47. Marshall, "Lobel," *Horn Book,* 326.

48. Quoted in *Third Book of Junior Authors* (New York: Wilson, 1972), 182.

49. Quoted in Rollin, "Astonished Witness," 196.

50. Quoted in David W. McCullough, "Eye on Books," *Book of the Month Club News,* August 1977, 20.

51. Anita Lobel, "Arnold at Home," *Horn Book* 57 (August 1981):410.

52. "Birthdays," *Theory,* 323.

53. See Richard Jenkyns, *The Victorians and Ancient Greece* (Cambridge: Harvard University Press, 1980).

54. George H. Ford, "Felicitous Space: The Cottage Controversy," in *Nature and the Victorian Imagination,* ed. U. C. Knoepflmacher and G. B. Tennyson (Berkeley: University of California Press, 1977), 24–48.

55. Emile Cammaerts, *The Poetry of Nonsense* (New York: Dutton, 1925), 25.

56. Elizabeth Sewell, *The Field of Nonsense* (London: Chatto & Windus, 1952), 111.

57. Sir Edward Strachey, introduction to *Edward Lear's Nonsense Omnibus* (London: Warne, 1943).

58. Quoted in Natov and DeLuca, "Interview," 91.

59. Quoted in Hood, "Crocodile's Terror," *Instructor,* 34.

60. Eleanor Terry Lincoln, introduction to *Pastoral and Romance: Modern Essays in Criticism,* ed. Eleanor Terry Lincoln (Englewood Cliffs, N.J.: Prentice-Hall, 1969), 3.

61. "The Evening Meal," in *The Scribner Anthology for Young People,* ed. Anne Diven (New York: Scribners, 1976), 194. "The Evening

Meal" was originally written by Lobel as a story for *Mouse Tales* and was one of the many he rejected as not working dramatically. When the mice were replaced by goats a few years later the drama worked.

62. John Donovan, "American Dispatch," *Signal*, no. 19 (January 1976): 43.

63. Suzanne Langer, *Feeling and Form* (New York: Scribners, 1953), 339.

64. *Arnold Lobel: Meet the Newbery Author Series*, rev. ed. (New York: Random House, 1986). A filmstrip-cassette.

65. "Frog," *Claremont*, 154.

Chapter Two

1. Quoted in Annalyn Swan, "An Aesop for Our Time," *Newsweek*, 18 August 1980, 78.

2. Quoted in Diane Roback, ed., "Arnold Lobel Remembered," *Publishers Weekly*, 29 January 1988, 395.

3. Quoted in McCullough, "Friends," 69.

4. Bernard Scharfstein, letter to author, 3 August 1987.

5. Quoted in Natov and DeLuca, "Interview," 73.

6. Quoted in Roback, "Lobel Remembered," 395.

7. Fred Phleger, letter to author, 27 August 1987.

8. Quoted in Natov and DeLuca, "Interview," 86.

9. Quoted in Rollin, "Astonished Witness," 194.

10. Ibid.

11. Quoted in David E. White, "Profile: Arnold Lobel." *Language Arts* 65 (September 1988):493.

12. Donnarae MacCann and Olga Richard, review of *Whiskers & Rhymes, Wilson Library Bulletin* 61 (May 1987): 47.

13. Alison Lurie, review of *The Random House Book of Mother Goose, New York Times Book Review*, 9 November 1986, 61.

14. Marshall, "Lobel," *Horn Book*, 328.

15. Ibid.

16. Quoted in *Books Are by People*, ed. Hopkins, 157.

17. Quoted in Rollin, "Astonished Witness," 195.

18. Quoted in White, "Profile," *Language Arts*, 492.

19. Arnold Lobel in conversation with author, New York, N.Y., 12 January 1987.

20. "Children's Book Illustrators Play Favorites," *Wilson Library Bulletin* 52 (October 1977): 167.

21. Quoted in "Natural Illustrator," *Early Years*, 103. Lobel speaks about his love of horror films and their "cozy fear" in greater depth in his last published interview: White, "Profile," *Language Arts*, 489–94.

22. Quoted in *Illustrators of Children's Books, 1957–1966,* ed. Lee Kingman et al. (Boston: Horn Book, 1968), 141.

23. Quoted in Diane Roback, "Arnold Lobel's Three Years with Mother Goose," *Publishers Weekly,* 22 August 1986, 32.

24. Quoted in Hands, *Illustrating,* 99.

25. "Favorites," *Wilson,* 165.

Chapter Three

1. Quoted in Rollin, "Astonished Witness," 194.

2. Quoted in *Books Are by People,* ed. Hopkins, 157.

3. *Arnold Lobel, Meet the Newbery Author,* rev. ed. (New York: Random House, 1986).

4. *A Zoo for Mister Muster* (New York: Harper & Row, 1962), 9.

5. George Woods, review of *A Zoo for Mister Muster, New York Times Book Review,* 13 May 1962, 5.

6. George Woods, review of *Prince Bertram the Bad, New York Times Book Review,* 12 May 1963, 5.

7. E. M. Graves, review of *Prince Bertram the Bad, Commonweal,* 24 May 1963, 255.

8. Review of *Prince Bertram the Bad, Christian Science Monitor,* 9 May 1963, B3.

9. Review of *Giant John, Junior Bookshelf* 29 (October 1965): 278.

10. Fritz Eichenberg, review of *Giant John, Book Week,* 1 November 1964, 26.

11. *Fables* (New York: Harper & Row, 1980), 11; hereafter cited parenthetically in the text as *F* followed by page number.

12. Quoted in Natov and DeLuca, "Interview," 86.

13. Quoted in "Natural Illustrator," *Early Years,* 34.

14. Virginia Makins, review of *The Bears of the Air, Times Educational Supplement* (London), 24 November 1978, 46.

15. Margaret Poarch, review of *The Bears of the Air, School Library Journal* 12 (September 1965):191.

16. Review of *The Bears of the Air, Junior Bookshelf* 31 (February 1967):33.

17. Richard Kluger, review of *The Bears of the Air, Book Week,* 31 October 1965, 16.

18. Quoted in McCullough, "Friends," 54.

19. George Woods, review of *Martha, the Movie Mouse, New York Times Book Review,* 25 September 1966, 34.

20. Elva Harmon, review of *Martha, the Movie Mouse, School Library Journal* 13 (September 1966):236.

21. Alice Dalgliesh, review of *Martha, the Movie Mouse, Saturday Review,* 17 September 1966, 41.

22. *Martha, the Movie Mouse* (New York: Harper & Row, 1966), 26.

23. Quoted in Rollin, "Astonished Witness," 195.

24. *The Great Blueness and Other Predicaments* (New York: Harper & Row, 1968), 29.

25. Eleanor Glaser, review of *The Great Blueness and Other Predicaments, School Library Journal* 15 (January 1969):287–88.

26. Selma G. Lanes, review of *The Great Blueness and Other Predicaments, New York Times Book Review,* 3 November 1968, 69.

27. *The Great Blueness and Other Predicaments* (final book dummy), Kerlan Collection.

28. George Woods, review of *Small Pig, New York Times Book Review,* 30 March 1969, 28.

29. Margery Fisher, review of *Small Pig, Growing Point* 9 (July 1970):1565.

Chapter Four

1. "Birthdays," *Theory,* 323.

2. "Favorites," *Wilson,* 167.

3. W. H. Auden, "Light Verse," in *The English Auden: Poems, Essays and Dramatic Writings, 1927–1939,* ed. Edward Mendelson (New York: Random House, 1977), 367.

4. "Favorites," *Wilson,* 167.

5. Selma G. Lanes, review of *The Comic Adventures of Old Mother Hubbard, New York Times Book Review,* 3 November 1968, 69.

6. Marshall, "Lobel," *Horn Book,* 327.

7. Cammaerts, *Nonsense,* 69.

8. Edward Lear, *The Complete Nonsense of Edward Lear,* ed. Holbrook Jackson (1947; reprint, New York: Dover, 1951), 103.

9. Cammaerts, *Nonsense,* 70.

10. Lobel provided a two-page illustration for the same verse in the 1983 *Random House Book of Poetry for Children* in addition to illustrations for "The Owl and the Pussycat" and two of Lear's limericks. Contrary to Alison Lurie's charge in the *New York Times Book Review,* Lobel's *Mother Goose* (1986) contains no texts by Lear.

11. Quoted in "Authors and Editors," *Publishers' Weekly,* 17 May 1971, 12.

12. Lear, *Complete Nonsense* (Dover reprint), 245.

13. Harve and Margot Zemach, review of *The New Vestments* by Edward Lear, *New York Times Book Review,* 21 June 1970, 22.

14. Vivien Noakes, *Edward Lear, 1812–1888* (New York: Abrams, 1986), 183.

15. *The Ice-Cream Cone Coot and Other Rare Birds* (New York: Parents, 1971), 12; hereafter cited parenthetically by page number in the text.

16. Marianne Hough, review of *The Ice-Cream Cone Coot and Other Rare Birds, School Library Journal* 18 (September 1971):134.

17. Elizabeth Minot Graves, review of *The Ice-Cream Cone Coot and Other Rare Birds, Commonweal,* 21 May 1971, 266.

18. Cammaerts, *Nonsense,* 41.

19. Quoted in Natov and DeLuca, "Interview," 90.

20. Arnold Lobel in conversation with author, New York, N. Y. 10 September 1987.

21. Noakes, *Lear,* 179. See also Donald J. Gray, "The Uses of Victorian Laughter," *Victorian Studies* 10 (1966):145–76.

22. Noakes, *Lear,* 180.

23. Zena Sutherland, review of *On the Day Peter Stuyvesant Sailed into Town, Bulletin of the Center for Children's Books* 25 (December 1971):60.

24. See Max Keith Sutton, "'Inverse Sublimity' in Victorian Humor," *Victorian Studies* 10 (1966):177–92.

25. *The Children's Book Showcase, 1975, Catalog* (New York: Children's Book Council, 1975), 41.

26. Lear, *Complete Nonsense,* 88.

27. *The Man Who Took the Indoors Out* (New York: Harper & Row, 1974), 15; hereafter cited parenthetically by page number in the text.

28. Yi-Fu Tuan, *Topophilia: A Study of Environmental Perception, Attitudes, and Values* (Englewood Cliffs, N.J.: Prentice-Hall, 1974), 99.

29. See Gray, "Laughter," *Victorian,* 145–76.

30. Lear, *Complete Nonsense,* 14.

31. Virginia Haviland, review of *The Man Who Took the Indoors Out, Horn Book* 50 (October 1974):131.

32. Brian Alderson, review of *The Man Who Took the Indoors Out, Children's Book Review* 6 (October 1976):27.

33. Quoted in Natov and DeLuca, "Interview," 79.

34. "Favorites," *Wilson,* 166.

35. Marcus Crouch, review of *Gregory Griggs and Other Nursery Rhyme People, School Library Journal* 27 (March 1979):36.

36. Review of *Gregory Griggs and Other Nursery Rhyme People, Junior Bookshelf* 43 (February 1979):20.

37. *Gregory Griggs and Other Nursery Rhyme People* (New York: Greenwillow, 1978), 48; hereafter cited parenthetically in the text as *GG* followed by page number.

158 ARNOLD LOBEL

38. Quoted in Rollin, "Astonished Witness," 192.

39. *The Book of Pigericks* (New York: Harper & Row, 1983), 11; hereafter cited parenthetically by page number in the text.

40. Lear, *Complete Nonsense,* 189.

41. Ibid. 204.

42. Ibid, 160.

43. "Favorites," *Wilson,* 167.

44. Cammaerts, *Nonsense,* 6.

45. See as an example Joyce Thomas, "'There Was an Old Man . . .': The Sense of Nonsense Verse," *Children's Literature Association Quarterly* 10 (Fall 1985):119–22.

46. Nancy Willard, "The Game and the Garden: The Lively Art of Nonsense," in *Angel in the Parlor: Five Stories and Eight Essays* (San Diego: Harcourt, 1983), 272.

47. "Meet Your Author," *Cricket* 5 (September 1977):9.

48. "A Good Picture Book," *Celebrating,* 74.

49. "Birthdays," *Theory,* 324.

50. "Favorites," *Wilson,* 167.

51. "Birthdays," *Theory,* 323.

52. Doris Orgel, review of *The Book of Pigericks, New York Times Book Review,* 8 May 1983, 37.

53. Donnarae MacCann and Olga Richard, review of *The Book of Pigericks, Wilson Library Bulletin* 57 (May 1983): 771.

54. Jennifer Dunning, "A Writer Breaking into Song," *New York Times,* 25 February 1983, C10. Lobel closed his evening by singing "Toad and Frog—Frog and Toad" written for him as a gift by friend and voice instructor, composer John Wallowitch.

55. Lynn Littlefield Hoopes, review of *Whiskers & Rhymes, Christian Science Monitor,* 1 November 1985, B6.

56. *Whiskers & Rhymes* (New York: Greenwillow, 1985), 28; hereafter cited parenthetically by page number in the text.

57. One of the songs Lobel sang during his evening at the West Bank Cabaret was a comic song he had written with John Wallowitch. Entitled "I Love You, Miss Streep," it told of a man so in love with her screen image that he watched her on videotape while his wife slept next to him.

58. Ethel L. Heins, review of *Whiskers & Rhymes, Horn Book* 62 (January/February 1986):67.

59. "Favorites," *Wilson,* 166.

60. Nancy Willard, review of *Whiskers & Rhymes, New York Times Book Review,* 10 November 1985, 36.

61. Thomas Carlyle, "Jean Paul Friedrich Richter," in *Critical and Miscellaneous Essays,* vol. 1 (New York: John Lovell, 1869), 17.

62. Wright Morris, *The Home Place* (New York: Scribners, 1948), 132–45.

63. *The Turnaround Wind* (New York: Harper & Row, 1988), 4; hereafter cited parenthetically by page number in the text.

64. Arnold Lobel in conversation with author, New York, N.Y., 10 September 1987.

65. Edward Lear, *Teapots and Quails and Other New Nonsense,* ed. Angus Davidson and Philip Hofer (London: John Murray, 1953), 54.

66. G. K. Chesterton, "How Pleasant to Know Mr. Lear," in *A Handful of Authors* (London: Sheed & Ward, 1953), 124.

67. "Favorites," *Wilson,* 166.

Chapter Five

1. *Grasshopper on the Road* (New York: Harper & Row, 1978), 52.

2. Ezra Pound, *A B C of Reading* (New Haven: Yale, 1934), xi.

3. Margery Fisher, review of *Frog and Toad Together, Growing Point* 12 (October 1973): 2229–30.

4. Quoted in McCullough, "Friends," 54.

5. Quoted in Natov and DeLuca, "Interview," 86.

6. In 1986 Lobel created a full-color poster of Frog and Toad flying a kite for The Peaceable Kingdom Press in Berkeley, California. While softer in mood than the pop-up illustrations, it remains bolder in color than the "I Can Read" volumes and yet evokes much of their warmth.

7. *Frog and Toad Together* (New York: Harper & Row, 1972), 6; hereafter cited parenthetically in the text as *FTT* followed by page number.

8. See Francis Haskell, *Past and Present in Art and Taste: Selected Essays* (New Haven: Yale, 1983), 155–74.

9. David Young, *The Heart's Forest: A Study of Shakespeare's Pastoral Plays* (New Haven: Yale, 1972), 31.

10. Lois Kuznets, "Toad Hall Revisited," *Children's Literature* 7 (1978):116.

11. Kenneth Grahame, "The Romance of the Road," in *Pagan Papers* (1898; reprint, Freeport, N.Y.: Books for Libraries Press, 1972), 15.

12. Martha Hale Shackford, "A Definition of the Pastoral Idyll," *PMLA* 19 (1904):586.

13. William Blake, *The Marriage of Heaven and Hell,* in *William Blake's Writing,* vol. 1, ed. G. E. Bentley, Jr. (Oxford: Clarendon Press, 1978), 82.

14. Eliot Fremont-Smith, review of *Frog and Toad All Year, New York Times Book Review,* 14 November 1976, 30.

15. Paul Alpers, *The Singer of the Ecologues: A Study of Virgilian Pastoral* (Berkeley: University of California Press, 1979), 215.

16. John Rouse, *The Completed Gesture: Myth, Character and Education* (New Jersey: Skyline, 1978), 12.

17. *Frog and Toad All Year* (Harper & Row, 1976), 53; hereafter cited parenthetically in the text as *FTAY* followed by page number.

18. Ronald A. Sharp, *Friendship and Literature: Spirit and Form* (Durham, N.C.: Duke University Press, 1986), 92.

19. Lore Metzger, *One Foot in Eden: Modes of Pastoral in Romantic Poetry* (Chapel Hill: University of North Carolina Press, 1986), xii.

20. Quoted in McCullough, "Friends," 69.

21. Sharp, *Friendship*, 37.

22. *Days with Frog and Toad* (New York: Harper & Row, 1979), 64.

23. Rosenmeyer, *Green Cabinet*, 97.

24. Quoted in Rollin, "Astonished Witness," 193.

25. Ibid.

26. Annie Dillard, *Living by Fiction* (New York: Harper & Row, 1982), 120.

27. Bernard N. Schilling, *The Comic Spirit: Boccaccio to Thomas Mann* (Detroit: Wayne State University Press, 1965), 11.

28. Quoted in Natov and DeLuca, "Interview," 84.

29. Quoted in White, "Profile," *Language Arts,* 490.

30. Rosenmeyer, *Green Cabinet*, 174.

31. Empson, *Some Versions of Pastoral*, 22.

32. Ibid., 81.

33. Quoted in Natov and DeLuca, "Interview," 94.

34. Quoted in White, "Profile," *Language Arts,* 490.

35. Quoted in Rollin, "Astonished Witness," 194.

36. Beatrix Potter, *The Roly-Poly Pudding* (New York: Warne, 1908), 59.

37. Beatrix Potter, *The Tale of Peter Rabbit* (New York: Warne, 1903), 10.

38. Kenneth Grahame, *The Wind in the Willows* (New York: Scribners, 1908), 232.

39. In his last published interview (to date) Lobel commented: "I was looking for two male characters. The idea of two male chums is so traditional in literature. For a speech, I once made a list of these: Rosencrantz and Guilderstein, the two guys from *Waiting for Godot,* Don Quixote and Sancho, Butch Cassidy and the Sundance Kid, etc. I wanted them to be alike, yet different." Quoted in White, "Profile," *Language Arts,* 490.

40. Christopher Bram, "Little Green Buddies," *Christopher Street,* May 1981, 61.

41. John Dewey, *Art as Experience* (1934; reprint, New York: Perigee Books, 1980), 48.

42. Quoted in Natov and DeLuca, "Interview," 95.

Chapter Six

1. Quoted in Swan, "Aesop," *Newsweek,* 78.

2. See Thomas Noel, *Theories of the Fable in the Eighteenth Century* (New York: Columbia University Press, 1975).

3. McNulty, "Children's Books for Christmas," New Yorker, 1 December, 1980, 212.

4. Swan, "Aesop," *Newsweek,* 78.

5. Paul Heins, review of *Fables, Horn Book* 56 (October 1980):520.

6. Review of *Fables, Kirkus Reviews,* 15 September 1980, 1229–30.

7. Patricia Dooley, review of *Fables, School Library Journal* 27 (October 1980):148.

8. Richard C. Tobias, *The Art of James Thurber* (Athens: Ohio University Press, 1969), 110.

9. Naomi Lewis, review of *Fables, Times Educational Supplement* (London), 16 January 1981, 31.

10. Ruth M. Stein, review of *Fables, Language Arts* 58 (May 1981):595.

11. *Aesop's Fables,* with drawings by Fritz Kredel (New York: Grosset & Dunlap, 1947), 169.

12. Florence Perry Heide and Sylvia Worth van Clief, *Fables You Shouldn't Pay Any Attention To* (Philadelphia: Lippincott, 1978), 19.

13. William Hugh Jansen, quoted by Daniel G. Hoffman in "Folklore in Literature: Notes toward a Theory of Interpretation," *Journal of American Folklore* 70 (1957):15–21.

14. *Aesop's Fables,* 115.

15. Ibid., 49, 55, 83, 113.

16. See Lloyd W. Daly, *Aesop without Morals* (New York: Thomas Yoseloff, 1961).

17. Joseph Jacobs, quoted by Thomas Newbigging in *Fables and Fabulists: Ancient and Modern* (1895; reprint, Freeport, N.Y.: Books for Libraries Press, 1972), 13.

18. Quoted in "Natural Illustrator," *Early Years,* 35.

19. Quoted in Hood, "Crocodile's Terror," *Instructor,* 35.

20. *Aesop's Fables,* 18, 25.

21. Quoted in Hood, "Crocodile's Terror," *Instructor,* 35.

22. Quoted in "Natural Illustrator," *Early Years,* 35.

23. Marie Winn, review of *Fables, New York Times Book Review,* 7 December 1980, 40.

24. Barbara Bader, "The Caldecott Spectrum," in *Newbery and Caldecott Medal Books, 1976–1985,* ed. Lee Kingman (Boston: Horn Book, 1986), 297.

25. Quoted in Brian Alderson, "Conversation with Medallion Winner," University of Southern Mississippi's Eighteenth Annual Children's Book Festival, 8 May 1985, De Grummond Collection (audio tape).

Chapter Seven

1. "Favorites," *Wilson,* 166.

2. Quoted in Natov and DeLuca, "Interview," 83.

3. *Mouse Tales* (New York: Harper & Row, 1972), 24.

4. Quoted in Natov and DeLuca, "Interview," 84.

5. Ibid.

6. Northrop Frye, *Anatomy of Criticism: Four Essays* (Princeton: Princeton University Press, 1957), 43.

7. Rosenmeyer, *Green Cabinet,* 177.

8. Quoted in McCullough, "Eye on Books," 20.

9. Ethel L. Heins, review of *Mouse Soup, Horn Book* 53 (June 1977):308.

10. "This Book Belongs to Me!," in *Once Upon a Time: Celebrating the Magic of Children's Books in Honor of the Twentieth Anniversary of Reading is Fundamental* (New York: Putnam, 1986), 38.

11. *Mouse Soup* (New York: Harper & Row, 1977), 62–64; hereafter cited parenthetically by page number in the text.

12. Gray, "Laughter," *Victorian,* 148.

13. Quoted in Rollin, "Astonished Witness," 194.

Chapter Eight

1. Quoted in Natov and DeLuca, "Interview," 74.

2. Nancy Willard, *Testimony of the Invisible Man: William Carlos Williams, Francis Ponge, Rainer Marie Rilke, Pablo Neruda* (Columbia: University of Missouri Press, 1970), 44.

3. Quoted in Natov and DeLuca, "Interview," 83.

4. *Owl at Home* (New York: Harper & Row, 1975), 28; hereafter cited parenthetically by page number in the text.

5. Rosenmeyer, *Green Cabinet,* 57.
6. Quoted in Natov and DeLuca, "Interview," 85.
7. White, *Stuart Little,* 92.
8. Sutton, "Sublimity," *Victorian,* 179.
9. Ibid.
10. G. K. Chesterton, "A Defence of Nonsense," in *The Defendent* (London: Dent, 1907), 69.
11. Gerald Mast, *The Comic Mind: Comedy and the Movies,* 2d ed. (Chicago: University of Chicago Press, 1979), 7.
12. *Grasshopper on the Road* (New York: Harper & Row, 1978), 15; hereafter cited parenthetically by page number in the text.
13. Wylie Sypher, "The Meanings of Comedy," in *Comedy,* ed. Wylie Sypher (Garden City: Doubleday, 1956), 245.
14. "A Good Picture Book," *Celebrating,* 77.
15. *Uncle Elephant* (New York: Harper & Row, 1981), 10; hereafter cited parenthetically by page number in the text.
16. Kenneth Grahame, "Prologue—The Olympians," in *The Golden Age* (1905; reprint, New York: Dodd, 1924), 8.
17. Swan, "Aesop," *Newsweek,* 78.
18. Quoted in Renato Poggioli, *The Oaten Flute: Essays on Pastoral Poetry and the Pastoral Ideal* (Cambridge: Harvard University Press, 1975), 40.
19. "A Good Picture Book," *Celebrating,* 77.

Chapter Nine

1. Quoted in Alderson, "Conversation," University of Southern Mississippi Children's Book Festival, De Grummond Collection.
2. Carl-Herman Tillhagen, translated and quoted in *Folktales and Society: Story-Telling in a Hungarian Peasant Community* by Linda Degh, trans. Emily M. Schossberger (Bloomington: Indiana University Press, 1969), 377.
3. Jansen quoted in "Interpretation," *Journal of American Folklore,* 15.
4. Sheryl B. Andrews, review of *Hansel and Gretel* by Wilhelm and Jacob Grimm, *Horn Book* 47 (April 1971):161.
5. Anne Pellowski, review of *Hansel and Gretel* by Wilhelm and Jacob Grimm, *New York Times Book Review,* 20 June 1971, 8.
6. Quoted in "Authors and Editors" *Publishers Weekly,* 17 May 1971, 11.
7. *On Market Street* (New York: Greenwillow, 1981), 34.
8. Quoted in *Junior Literary Guild Catalog,* March 1984, 17.

9. Roger Swain, review of *The Rose in My Garden, New York Times Book Review,* 1 April 1984, 29.

10. Natalie Babbitt, review of *Ming Lo Moves the Mountain, Book World—Washington Post,* 9 May 1982, 17.

11. Quoted in *Illustrators, 1957–1966,* ed. Kingman, 141.

12. Willard, "Garden," *Angel in the Parlor,* 261.

13. Quoted in Roback, "Mother Goose," 32.

14. Ibid., 33.

15. Ibid., 32.

16. Quoted in Alderson, "Conversation," University of Southern Mississippi, Children's Book Festival, De Grummond Collection.

17. Quoted in Roback, "Mother Goose," 33.

Chapter Ten

1. Quoted in Bea J. Pepan, "Author Meets His Fans—All Children," *Milwaukee Journal,* 25 April 1974, 5, part 2.

2. June Jordan, "Young People: Victims of Realism in Books and in Life," *Wilson Library Bulletin* 48 (October 1973): 144.

3. C. S. Lewis, "William Morris," in *Rehabilitations and Other Essays* (London: Oxford University Press, 1939), 49.

4. William Blake, *William Blake's Writing,* ed. Bentley, 36.

5. Ronald Paulson, "Hogarth and the English Garden: Visual and Verbal Structures," in *Encounters: Essays on Literature and the Visual Arts,* ed. John Dixon Hunt (New York: Norton, 1971), 90.

6. John Dixon Hunt, *The Figure in the Landscape: Poetry, Painting, and Gardening During the Eighteenth Century* (Baltimore: Johns Hopkins Press, 1976), xii.

7. Alexander Pope, *The Correspondence of Alexander Pope,* vol. 2, ed. George Sherburn (Oxford: Clarendon Press, 1956), 328.

8. "A Good Picture Book, *Celebrating,* 76.

9. Walter Benjamin, "The Storyteller," in *Illuminations,* trans. Harry Zohn (1955; New York: Schocken, 1968), 108.

Selected Bibliography

Primary Works

Books

The Bears of the Air. New York: Harper & Row, 1965.
The Book of Pigericks. New York: Harper & Row, 1983.
Days with Frog and Toad. New York: Harper & Row, 1979.
Fables. New York: Harper & Row, 1980.
Frog and Toad All Year. New York: Harper & Row, 1976.
Frog and Toad Are Friends. New York: Harper & Row, 1970.
Frog and Toad Coloring Book. New York: Harper & Row, 1981.
The Frog and Toad Pop-Up Book. New York: Harper & Row, 1986.
Frog and Toad Together. New York: Harper & Row, 1972.
Giant John. New York: Harper & Row, 1964.
Grasshopper on the Road. New York: Harper & Row, 1978.
The Great Blueness and Other Predicaments. New York: Harper & Row, 1968.
A Holiday for Mister Muster. New York: Harper & Row, 1963.
How the Rooster Saved the Day. Illustrated by Anita Lobel. New York: Greenwillow, 1977.
The Ice-Cream Cone Coot and Other Rare Birds. New York: Parents, 1971.
Lucille. New York: Harper & Row, 1964.
The Man Who Took the Indoors Out. New York: Harper & Row, 1974.
Martha, the Movie Mouse. New York: Harper & Row, 1966.
Ming Lo Moves the Mountain. New York: Greenwillow, 1982.
Mouse Soup. New York: Harper & Row, 1977.
Mouse Tales. New York: Harper & Row, 1972.
On Market Street. Illustrated by Anita Lobel. New York: Greenwillow, 1981.
On the Day Peter Stuyvesant Sailed into Town. New York: Harper & Row, 1971.
Owl at Home. New York: Harper & Row, 1975.
Prince Bertram the Bad. New York: Harper & Row, 1963.

The Rose in My Garden. Illustrated by Anita Lobel. New York: Greenwillow, 1984.
Small Pig. New York: Harper & Row, 1969.
A Treeful of Pigs. Illustrated by Anita Lobel. New York: Greenwillow, 1979.
The Turnaround Wind. New York: Harper & Row, 1988.
Uncle Elephant. New York: Harper & Row, 1981.
Whiskers & Rhymes. New York: Greenwillow, 1985.
A Zoo for Mister Muster. New York: Harper & Row, 1962.

Stories and Verse

"The Evening Meal." In *The Scribner Anthology for Young People,* edited by Anne Diven, 192–94. New York: Scribners, 1976.
"The Great Rabbit Circus." *Humpty Dumpty Magazine,* January 1968.
"Owls Old and Odd." *Humpty Dumpty Magazine,* January 1967.
"Very Strange Birds." *Humpty Dumpty Magazine,* February 1970.

Illustrations for Other Authors

All About Jewish Holidays and Customs by Morris Epstein. New York: Ktav, 1959.
Ants Are Fun by Mildred Myrick. New York: Harper & Row, 1968.
As I Was Crossing Boston Common by Norma Farber. New York: Dutton, 1975.
As Right as Right Can Be by Anne Rose. New York: Dial, 1976.
Bear All Year: A Guessing-Game Story by Harriet Ziefert. New York: Harper & Row, 1986.
Bear Gets Dressed: A Guessing-Game Story by Harriet Ziefert. New York: Harper & Row, 1986.
Bear Goes Shopping: A Guessing-Game Story by Harriet Ziefert. New York: Harper & Row, 1986.
Bear's Busy Morning: A Guessing-Game Story by Harriet Ziefert. New York: Harper & Row, 1986.
Benny's Animals and How He Put Them in Order by Millicent Selsam. New York: Harper & Row, 1966.
Bibletime: With 14 Full-Page Bible Pasteups and 84 Full-Color Perforated Bible Stamps by Sol Scharfstein. New York: Ktav, 1958.
Book of Chanukah: Poems, Riddles, Stories, Songs and Things to Do by Edythe Scharfstein. Illustrated with Ezekiel Schloss. New York: Ktav, 1959.
Circus by Jack Prelutsky. New York: Macmillan, 1974.

The Clay Pot Boy by Cynthia Jameson. New York: Coward, 1973.

The Comic Adventures of Old Mother Hubbard and Her Dog. Englewood Cliffs, N.J.: Bradbury, 1968.

The Devil and Mother Crump by Valerie Scho Carey. New York: Harper & Row, 1987.

Dinosaur Time by Peggy Parish. New York: Harper & Row, 1974.

Dudley Pippin by Phil Ressner. New York: Harper & Row, 1965.

The Four Little Children Who Went Around the World by Edward Lear. New York: Macmillan, 1968.

Gregory Griggs and Other Nursery Rhyme People. Edited by Arnold Lobel. New York: Greenwillow, 1978.

Good Ethan by Paula Fox. Scarsdale, N.Y.: Bradbury, 1973.

Greg's Microscope by Millicent Selsam. New York: Harper & Row, 1963.

Hansel and Gretel. Told by Jacob and Wilhelm Grimm. New York: Delacorte, 1971.

The Headless Horseman Rides Tonight: More Poems to Trouble Your Sleep by Jack Prelutsky. New York: Greenwillow, 1980.

Hebrew Dictionary: Activity Funbook by Sol Scharfstein. New York: Ktav, 1958.

Hildilid's Night by Cheli D. Ryan. New York: Macmillan, 1971.

Holiday Dictionary: With 90 Religious Objects to Color and 84 Full-Page Color Perforated Religious Objects Stamps by Sol Scharfstein. New York: Ktav, 1958.

Holidays Are Nice: Around the Year with the Jewish Child by Robert Garvey. Illustrated with Ezekiel Schloss. New York: Ktav, 1960.

I'll Fix Anthony by Judith Viorst. New York: Harper & Row, 1969.

Junk Day on Juniper Street and Other Easy to Read Stories by Lilian Moore. New York: Parents, 1969.

Let's Be Early Settlers with Daniel Boone by Peggy Parish. New York: Harper & Row, 1967.

Let's Be Indians by Peggy Parish. New York: Harper & Row, 1962.

Let's Get Turtles by Millicent Selsam. New York: Harper & Row, 1965.

"Little King Pippin." In "A Mother Goose Portfolio," in *Innocence and Experiences: Essays and Conversations on Children's Literature,* compiled and edited by Barbara Harrison and Gregory Maguire, 397. New York: Lothrop, 1987.

Little Runner of the Longhouse by Betty Baker. New York: Harper & Row, 1962.

The Magic Spectacles and Other Easy to Read Stories by Lilian Moore. New York: Parents, 1966.

The Master of Miracle by Sulamith Ish-Kishor. New York: Harper & Row, 1971.

The Mean Old Mean Hyena by Jack Prelutsky. New York: Greenwillow, 1978.

Merry Merry FIBruary by Doris Orgel. New York: Parents, 1977.
The Microscope by Maxine Kumin. New York: Harper & Row, 1984.
Miss Suzy by Miriam Young. New York: Parents, 1964.
Miss Suzy's Birthday by Miriam Young. New York: Parents, 1974.
Miss Suzy's Easter Surprise by Miriam Young. New York: Parents, 1972.
More Tales of Oliver Pig by Jean Van Leeuwen. New York: Dial, 1981.
My First Book of Prayers by Edythe Scharfstein. Illustrated with Ezekiel Schloss. New York: Ktav, 1958.
The New Vestments by Edward Lear. Englewood Cliffs, N.J.: Bradbury, 1970.
Nightmares: Poems to Trouble Your Sleep by Jack Prelutsky. New York: Greenwillow, 1976.
Oscar Otter by Nathaniel Benchley. New York: Harper & Row, 1966.
The Quarreling Book by Charlotte Zolotow. New York: Harper & Row, 1963.
The Random House Book of Mother Goose: A Treasure of 306 Timeless Nursery Rhymes. Selected by Arnold Lobel. New York: Random House, 1986.
The Random House Book of Poetry for Children. Edited by Jack Prelutsky. New York: Random House, 1983.
Red Fox and His Canoe by Nathaniel Benchley. New York: Harper & Row, 1964.
Red Tag Comes Back by Fred Phleger. New York: Harper & Row, 1961.
Sam, the Minuteman by Nathaniel Benchley. New York: Harper & Row, 1969.
Seahorse by Robert Morris. New York: Harper & Row, 1972.
The Secret Three by Mildred Myrick. New York: Harper & Row, 1963.
Sing a Song of Popcorn: Every Child's Book of Poems. Selected by Beatrice Schenk de Regniers et al. Illustrated with Marcia Brown, Leo and Diane Dillon, Richard Egielski, Trina Schart Hyman, Maurice Sendak, Marc Simont, and Margot Zemach. New York: Scholastic, 1988.
Someday by Charlotte Zolotow. New York: Harper & Row, 1965.
Something Old, Something New by Susan Oneacre Rinehart. New York: Harper & Row, 1961.
Star Thief by Andrea DiNoto. New York: Macmillan, 1967.
The Strange Disappearance of Arthur Cluck by Nathaniel Benchley. New York: Harper & Row, 1967.
The Tale of Meshka the Kvetch by Carol Chapman. New York: Dial, 1980.
Tales of Oliver Pig by Jean Van Leeuwen. New York: Dial, 1979.
The Terrible Tiger by Jack Prelutsky. New York: Macmillan, 1969.
Terry and the Caterpillars by Millicent Selsam. New York: Harper & Row, 1962.

A Three Hat Day by Laura Geringer. New York: Harper & Row, 1985.
Tot Botot and His Little Flute by Laura Cathon. New York: Macmillan, 1970.
Tyrannosaurus Was a Beast by Jack Prelutsky. New York: Greenwillow, 1988.
Where's the Cat? by Harriet Ziefert. New York: Harper & Row, 1987.
Where's the Dog? by Harriet Ziefert. New York: Harper & Row, 1987.
Where's the Guinea Pig? by Harriet Ziefert. New York: Harper & Row, 1987.
Where's the Turtle? by Harriet Ziefert. New York: Harper & Row, 1987.
The Witch on the Corner by Felice Holman. New York: Norton, 1966.

Essays and Speeches

"Birthdays and Beginnings." *Theory into Practice* 21 (Autumn 1982):322–24.
"Caldecott Medal Acceptance." *Horn Book* 57 (August 1981):400–4.
"Children's Book Illustrators Play Favorites." *Wilson Library Bulletin* 57 (October 1977):165–68.
"Frog and Toad: A Short History." *Claremont Reading Conference Yearbook* 42 (1978):147–54.
"A Good Picture Book Should. . . ." In *Celebrating Children's Books: Essays on Children's Literature in Honor of Zena Sutherland*, edited by Betsy Hearne and Marilyn Kaye, 73–80. New York: Lothrop, 1981.
"Show Me the Way to Go Home." *Horn Book* 65 (January/February 1989): 26–29.

Autobiographical Sketches

"Arnold Lobel." In *Illustrators of Children's Books 1957–1966*, edited by Lee Kingman et al., 141. Boston: Horn Book, 1968.
"Arnold Lobel." In *Something about the Author*, vol. 6, edited by Anne Commire, 147–48. Detroit: Gale Research, 1974.
"Arnold Lobel." In *Third Book of Junior Authors*, edited by Doris de Montreville and Donna Hill, 181–82. New York: Wilson, 1972.
Junior Literary Guild Catalog, March 1984, 17.
"Meet Your Author." *Cricket* 5 (September 1977):9.
"This Book Belongs to Me!" In *Once upon a Time: Celebrating the Magic of Children's Books in Honor of the Twentieth Anniversary of Reading is Fundamental*, 38–39. New York: Putnam, 1986.

Interviews

"Anita and Arnold Lobel." In *Books are by People,* edited by Lee Bennett Hopkins, 156–59. New York: Citation Press, 1969.

Arnold Lobel: Meet the Newbery Author Series. Rev. ed. New York: Random House, 1986. Filmstrip cassette.

"Arnold Lobel . . . the Natural Illustrator . . . the Entertainer." *Early Years* 11 (November 1980):34–35, 103.

"Authors and Editors." *Publishers Weekly,* 17 May 1971, 11–13.

Dunning, Jennifer. "A Writer Breaking into Song." *New York Times,* 25 February 1983, C10.

Hood, Susan. "A Crocodile's Terror and an Elephant's Error—That's What Arnold Lobel's *Fables* Are Made Of!" *Instructor* 90 (May 1981):34–35.

Lewis, Pamela. "Fables of Their Own Making." *Houston Post,* 12 April 1981, 3BB.

McCullough, David W. "Arnold Lobel and Friends." *New York Times Book Review,* 11 November 1979, 54, 69.

———. "Eye on Books." *Book of the Month Club News,* August 1977, 20.

McNulty, Faith. "Children's Books for Christmas." *New Yorker,* 1 December 1980, 212.

Natov, Roni, and Geraldine DeLuca. "An Interview with Arnold Lobel." *Lion and the Unicorn* 1 (1977):72–97.

Pepan, Bea J. "Author Meets His Fans—All Children." *Milwaukee Journal,* 25 April 1974, 5 sec. 2.

Roback, Diane. "Arnold Lobel's Three Years with Mother Goose." *Publishers Weekly,* 22 August 1986, 32–33.

Rollin, Lucy. "The Astonished Witness Disclosed: An Interview with Arnold Lobel." *Children's Literature in Education* 15 (Winter 1984):192–97.

Swan, Annalyn. "An Aesop for Our Time." *Newsweek,* 18 August 1980, 78.

White, David E. "Profile: Arnold Lobel." *Language Arts* 65 (September 1988):489–94.

Secondary Works

Biographical Sketches

Gordon, Elizabeth. "Arnold Lobel." In *Newbery and Caldecott Medal Books 1976–1985,* edited by Lee Kingman, 226–28, Boston: Horn Book, 1986.

Hirschman, Susan. "Arnold Lobel." *Horn Book* 64 (May/June 1988):324–25.
Lobel, Anita. "Arnold at Home." *Horn Book* 57 (August 1981):405–10.
Marshall, James, "Arnold Lobel." *Horn Book* 64 (May/June 1988):326–28.

Miscellany

Hale, Robert E. "Musings." *Horn Book* 63 (May/June 1987):323–25.
Hearn, Michael Patrick. "Arnold Lobel: An Appreciation." *Book World,* 10 January 1988, 7, 12.
Silvey, Anita. "Caldecott's Heirs." *Horn Book* 63 (November/December 1987):693.
Roback, Diane, ed. "Arnold Lobel Remembered." *Publishers Weekly,* 29 January 1988, 395. Contributors: John Donovan, Elizabeth Gordon, Susan Hirschman, James Marshall, Katherine Paterson, Jack Prelutsky, Maurice Sendak, and Frank Sloan.

Criticism

Babbitt, Natalie. "Fairy Tales and Far-Flung Places." Review of *Ming Lo Moves the Mountain. Book World—Washington Post,* 9 May 1982, 16–17.
Boudreau, Ingeborg. Review of *Frog and Toad Together. New York Times Book Review,* 7 May 1972, 37.
Bram, Christopher. "Little Green Buddies." *Christopher Street,* May 1981, 59–61.
Donovan, John. "American Dispatch." Review of *Owl at Home. Signal,* January 1976, 43.
Fisher, Margery. Review of *Frog and Toad Are Friends. Growing Point* 10 (October 1971):1802.
———. Review of *Frog and Toad Together. Growing Point* 12 (October 1973):2229–30.
———. Review of *Owl at Home. Growing Point* 15 (October 1976):2966.
Fremont-Smith, Eliot. Review of *Frog and Toad All Year. New York Times Book Review,* 14 November 1976, 30, 32.
Gmuca, Jacqueline. "Arnold Lobel." In *American Writers for Children since 1960: Poets, Illustrators, and Nonfiction Authors,* edited by Glenn E. Estes, 165–76, Detroit: Gale Research, 1987.
———. "Arnold Lobel." In *Twentieth-Century Children's Writers,* 492–93. New York: St. Martins Press, 1983.

Heins, Ethel L. Review of *Whiskers & Rhymes*. *Horn Book* 62 (January/February 1986):67.

Herman, Gertrude. "A Picture is Worth Several Hundred Words." Review of *Grasshopper on the Road*. *Horn Book* 63 (January/February 1987):97.

———. "A Picture is Worth Several Hundred Words." Review of *The Random House Book of Mother Goose*. *Horn Book* 64 (January/February 1988):93.

Kuskin, Karla. "The Complete Illustrator." Review of *Ming Lo Moves the Mountain*. *New York Times Book Review*, 25 April 1982, 31, 46.

Lurie, Alison. "Roly-poly Fun and Feasting." Review of *The Random House Book of Mother Goose*. *New York Times Book Review*, 9 November 1986, 37, 61.

MacCann, Donnarae, and Olga, Richard. Review of *The Book of Pigericks*. *Wilson Library Bulletin* 52 (May 1983):771.

———. Review of *Fables*. *Wilson Library Bulletin*, 55 (April 1981):610.

———. Review of *Whiskers & Rhymes*. *Wilson Library Bulletin* 61 (May 1987):47.

Orgel, Doris. Review of *The Book of Pigericks*. *New York Times Book Review*, 8 May 1983, 37.

Richard, Olga, and Donnarae MacCann. Review of *Grasshopper on the Road*. *Wilson Library Bulletin* 53 (December 1978):338.

———. Review of *Ming Lo Moves the Mountain*. *Wilson Library Bulletin* 57 (January 1983):417.

Senick, Gerard J., ed. "Arnold Lobel." In *Children's Literature Review: Excerpts from Reviews, Criticism and Commentary on Books for Children*, 157–76. Detroit: Gale Research, 1983.

Willard, Nancy. "Pickle Paste and Winged Armchairs." Review of *Whiskers & Rhymes*. *New York Times Book Review*, 10 November 1985, 36.

Winn, Marie. Review of *Fables*. *New York Times Book Review*, 7 December 1980, 40.

Books and Essays

Bachelard, Gaston. *The Poetics of Space*. Translated by Maria Jolas. Boston: Beacon Press, 1969.

Calhoun, Blue. *The Pastoral Vision of William Morris: The Earthly Paradise*. Athens: University of Georgia Press, 1975.

Cammaerts, Emile. *The Poetry of Nonsense*. New York: Dutton, 1925.

Cody, Richard. *The Landscape of the Mind: Pastoralism and Platonic Theory in Tasso's "Aminta" and Shakespeare's Early Comedies*. Oxford: Clarendon Press, 1969.

Corrigan, Robert W., ed. *Comedy: Meaning and Form.* San Francisco: Chandler, 1965.

Empson, William. *Some Versions of Pastoral.* 1950. Reprint. New York: New Directions, 1974.

Gray, Donald J. "Humor as Poetry in Nineteenth-Century English Criticism." *Journal of English and Germanic Philology* 61 (1962):249–57.

———. "The Uses of Victorian Laughter." *Victorian Studies* 10 (1966):145–76.

Hunt, John Dixon. *The Figure in the Landscape: Poetry, Painting, and Gardening During the Eighteenth Century.* Baltimore: Johns Hopkins University Press, 1976.

Koppes, Phyllis Bixler. "The Child in Pastoral Myth: A Study in Rousseau and Wordsworth, Children's Literature and Literary Fantasy." Ph.D. diss., University of Kansas, 1977.

Lincoln, Eleanor Terry, ed. *Pastoral and Romance: Modern Essays in Criticism.* Englewood Cliffs, N.J.: Prentice-Hall, 1969.

Mast, Gerald. *The Comic Mind: Comedy and the Movies.* 2d ed. Chicago: University of Chicago Press, 1979.

Newbigging, Thomas. *Fables and Fabulists: Ancient and Modern.* 1895. Reprint. Freeport, N.Y.: Books for Libraries, 1972.

Noakes, Vivien. *Edward Lear 1812–1888.* New York: Abrams, 1986.

Noel, Thomas. *Theories of the Fable in the Eighteenth Century.* New York: Columbia University Press, 1975.

Rosenmeyer, Thomas G. *The Green Cabinet: Theocritus and the European Pastoral Lyric.* Berkeley: University of California Press, 1969.

Sewell, Elizabeth. *The Field of Nonsense.* London: Chatto & Windus, 1952.

Sharp, Ronald A. *Friendship and Literature: Spirit and Form.* Durham, N.C.: Duke University Press, 1986.

Stewart, Susan. *Nonsense: Aspects of Intertextuality in Folklore and Literature.* Baltimore: Johns Hopkins University Press, 1979.

Sutton, Max Keith. "'Inverse Sublimity' in Victorian Humor." *Victorian Studies* 10 (1966):177–92.

Willard, Nancy. "The Game and the Garden: The Lively Art of Nonsense." In *Angel in the Parlor: Five Stories and Eight Essays,* 258–82. San Diego: Harcourt, 1983.

Young, David. *The Heart's Forest: A Study of Shakespeare's Pastoral Plays.* New Haven: Yale University Press, 1972.

Index

About the Author

George Shannon received his B.S. from Western Kentucky University and his M.S.L.S. from the University of Kentucky. He has worked as both a school and public librarian and a professional storyteller, and has been a visiting writer in schools stretching from El Paso to the Arctic Circle. He speaks at children's literature conferences around the country and has delivered papers at the Modern Language Association, the Children's Literature Association, and the National Council of Teachers of English. His critical essays concerning children's literature have appeared in *Horn Book, Children's Literature Association Quarterly,* and *Children's Literature in Education.* He is also the author of several picture books including *The Surprise* (1983), *Sea Gifts* (1989), and *Dancing the Breeze* (1990), and a young adult novel, *Unlived Affections* (1989). He lives in Eau Claire, Wisconsin.